THE
GOD OF THE WITCHES

by

MARGARET A. MURRAY

Look unto the rock whence ye are hewn,
and to the hole of the pit whence ye are
digged.

ISAIAH, li, I

OXFORD UNIVERSITY PRESS
LONDON   OXFORD   NEW YORK

OXFORD UNIVERSITY PRESS

Oxford   London   Glasgow

New York   Toronto   Melbourne   Wellington

Nairobi   Dar es Salaam   Cape Town

Kuala Lumpur   Singapore   Jakarta   Hong Kong   Tokyo

Delhi   Bombay   Calcutta   Madras   Karachi

First published by Sampson Low, Marston and Co., Ltd., 1931

Reissued by Oxford University Press, New York,
and Faber and Faber, Ltd., London, 1952

First issued as an Oxford University Press paperback, by special
arrangement with Faber and Faber, Ltd., 1970

This reprint, 1979

PRINTED IN THE UNITED STATES OF AMERICA

Contents

Illustrations

Foreword

This book being intended for the general reader as well as for the student of anthropology the authority for each statement is not always given in the text. For the benefit of those who wish to pursue the study further there is a bibliography for each chapter at the end of the book. For a complete bibliography of English records the reader is referred to Wallace Notestein's *History of Witchcraft in England* (Washington, 1911). In my *Witch Cult in Western Europe* (Oxford University Press, 1921) the bibliography is chiefly of the British Isles, France, Belgium, and Sweden.

Though I am concerned with the existence through the Middle Ages of a primitive religion in western Europe only, there is no doubt that the cult was spread in early times through central and eastern Europe and the Near East. There it survived, underlying, as in the West, the official religion of the country, Christianity in Europe, Islam and sometimes Christianity in the East. The *literati* of those countries were of the faith there in the ascendant, consequently the Old Religion was seldom recorded, for Paganism belonged there as here to the inarticulate uneducated masses who remained for many centuries untouched by the new religion. I have not attempted to give every known instance of the beliefs and ritual of the 'witches'; all I desire to do is to present to the reader a fairly complete view of the cult from contemporary evidence. I have also, as occasion arose, compared the Witch-Cult with other religions of ancient and modern times.

My grateful thanks are due to my sister, Mrs. M. E. Slater, and to Mr. G. A. Wainwright for much kind help and many valuable suggestions; to Mr. F. Rutter, Town-

Foreword

clerk of Shaftesbury, for the information which he so kindly furnished concerning the Prize Besom.

In this second edition the original matter remains unaltered, but several additions have been made. These include the account of that interesting survival of a primitive rite, the Puck Fair of co. Kerry (p. 43), for which I am indebted to Mrs. Percival-Maxwell; the whole of chapter VI (pp. 145–59); and the suggestion as to the meaning of the *Face of Lucca* in the oath of William Rufus. One new illustration has been added, the frontispiece, which shows Joan of Arc identifying the Dauphin. This is taken from a miniature painting in a fifteenth-century manuscript of Enguerrand de Moustrelet (Brit. Mus. Royal MS. 20 Dviii f 7). It is so nearly contemporary with Joan that it is possibly a truthful portrait, for it was painted within the memory of many who, like de Moustrelet himself, had actually seen her.

M. A. MURRAY

Introduction

Much has been written of late years on the changes, evolution, and continuity of material culture from the Palaeolithic period down to the Roman era when written accounts of Western Europe began. The movements of peoples, the increase of trade, the advance of civilization, have all been traced with considerable precision. The late Palaeolithic period of Europe has been linked with the Capsian, which is of African origin, and the gulf between the Palaeolithic and Neolithic civilizations is being rapidly bridged. The material side of life has received most attention, for the concrete remains of Early Man are very numerous. The pictorial and plastic arts of the most remote periods have also been studied, and from the arts and handicrafts the mental development of the Palaeolithic and Neolithic peoples can be traced. But the religion of those early times has been entirely neglected, with the exception of a few references to Mother-goddesses and to burial customs. The student of early religion begins his subject in the early Bronze Age of the Near East and totally ignores Western Europe in the Stone Ages; he ends his study with the introduction of Christianity, as the study of that religion is known as Theology. There is, however, a continuity of belief and ritual which can be traced from the Palaeolithic period down to modern times. It is only by the anthropological method that the study of religions, whether ancient or modern, can be advanced.

The attitude of all writers towards the post-Christian era

in Europe, especially towards the Middle Ages, has been that of the ecclesiastic, the historian, the artist, the scholar, or the economist. Hitherto the anthropologist has confined himself to the pre-Christian periods or to the modern savage. Yet medieval Europe offers to the student of Mankind one of the finest fields of research. In this volume I have followed one line only of anthropological inquiry, the survival of an indigenous European cult and the interaction between it and the exotic religion which finally overwhelmed it. I have traced the worship of the Horned God onwards through the centuries from the Palaeolithic prototypes, and I have shown that the survival of the cult was due to the survival of the races who adored that god, for this belief could not have held its own against the invasions of other peoples and religions unless a stratum of the population were strong enough to keep it alive.

If the evidence is carefully examined it becomes clear that this stratum consisted of the descendants of the Palaeolithic, Neolithic, and Bronze Age races. The Palaeolithic people were hunters, the Neolithic and Bronze Age people were pastoral and agricultural. Among all these races the Horned God was pre-eminent, for alike to hunting and pastoral folk animals were essential for life. After the general introduction of agriculture, the Horned God remained as a great deity, and was not dethroned even by the coming of the Iron Age. It was not till the rise of Christianity, with its fundamental doctrine that a non-Christian deity was a devil, that the cult of the Horned God fell into disrepute.

The idea of dividing the Power Beyond into two, one good and one evil, belongs to an advanced and sophisticated religion. In the more primitive cults the deity is in himself the author of all, whether good or bad. The monotheism of early religions is very marked, each little settlement or group of settlements having its one deity, male or female, whose power was co-terminous with that of his worshippers. Polytheism appears to have arisen with the amalgamation of tribes, each with its own deity. When a tribe whose deity was male coalesced with a tribe whose deity was female, the union of the peoples was symbolized in their religion by the marriage of their gods. When by peaceful infiltration a new god ousted an old one, he was said to be the son of his predecessor. But when the invasion was warlike the conquering deity was invested with all good attributes while the god of the vanquished took a lower place and was regarded by the conquerors as the producer of evil, and was consequently often more feared than their own legitimate deity. In ancient Egypt the fall from the position of a high god to that of a 'devil' is well exemplified in the god Setekh, who in early times was as much a giver of all good as Osiris, but later was so execrated that, except in the city of his special cult, his name and image were rigorously destroyed. In the study of the Horned God this fact of the fall from godship to devildom must be borne in mind.

Little is known of Palaeolithic Man beyond his flint tools, his painted and sculptured caves, his engraved bones, and a few skulls. He lived in caves in glacial conditions as is shown by the animals found with him. It is certain that there was some kind of ceremony, religious or magical, in which a horned man, presumably a god, took the leading part. It is equally certain that there must have been a worship of the female principle, but in the cult of the Horned God this does not appear till a much later stage.

Of the religion of the Neolithic period nothing is known in Western Europe except the burial rites. The gods have left no recognizable trace, though certain female figures may possibly represent goddesses. But when the Bronze Age arose the Horned God is found through all Europe from East to West. The fierce tribes who brought in the Iron Age destroyed the greater part of the previous civilization, and possibly the previous inhabitants also, except those descendants of the Neolithic and Bronze Age folk still remaining on the moors and downs, where agriculture was unsuitable at the time and where the valley people would be afraid to venture. Powerless though the moormen were against the new weapons they seem to have struck terror into the invaders. If there was war between the two races it was a guerrilla warfare, in which the Little People had the advantage over the slow-moving agriculturists. In the end a certain amount of intercourse must have been established. Whether it was due to trade and intermarriage that the worship of the Horned God was reintroduced among the tillers of the soil; or, as is more likely, that the people of the Iron Age had acquired the cult in their own habitat or in their slow march across Europe, it is certain that he retained his position as a high god.

It is not unlikely that at this period the cross was used by the conquerors as a magical method of frightening and scaring away the hill-people. The cross was already in use as a sacred symbol in the Bronze Age in Eastern Europe, and to the Iron Age belongs the Whiteleaf Cross cut in the chalk of the Chiltern hills, where it could exercise its protective power against the upland dwellers. In all accounts of fairies and witches it is only the cross that has power against them, the most sacred of other Christian objects and emblems had no effect. As late as the seventeenth century Sinistrari d'Ameno states that it is 'a most marvellous and incomprehensible fact that the Incubi do not obey the Exorcists, have no dread of exorcisms, no reverence for holy things, at the approach of which they are not in the least overawed . . . Incubi stand all these ordeals' (which drive away evil spirits) 'without taking to flight or showing the least fear; sometimes they laugh at exorcisms, strike the Exorcists themselves, and rend the sacred vestments'.[1] He therefore concluded that they were mortal and had souls like men. The evidence appears fairly conclusive that the deep-seated dread of the cross does not refer to the Christian symbol but dates back to a period several centuries before Christianity.

The Roman religion took no hold on Great Britain and was little regarded in Gaul. The Romans called the British and Gaulish deities by Roman names, but the religion was not Romanized, and no Roman god was ever completely

2. MASKED MAN WITH STAG'S ANTLERS

Palaeolithic painting, Caverne des Trois Freres, Ariege

3. MASKED DANCER

Palaeolithic Engraving from the Fourneau du Diable,
Dordogne

established in the West of Europe. The old deities continued in full force unaffected by foreign influence. The temple built on the summit of the Puy de Dome was dedicated to a god called by the Romans Mercurius, to his worshippers he was known as Dumus; Cernunnos, in spite of his Latinized name, was found in all parts of Gaul. Few of the names of the indigenous deities of Great Britain have survived, and the ritual received scant attention from the Roman recorders.

When Christianity first arrived in Great Britain it came in from the West and established itself among the people rather than the rulers. Centuries later other missionaries entered on the East. The Christian Church had by this time become more organized, more dogmatic, more bent on proselytizing. The main attack, therefore, was not on the people but on the royal families, particularly on the queens whose influence was well understood. Paganism, however, received continual reinforcements in the successive invasions of heathen peoples; Danes, Norsemen, Angles, Jutes, and Saxons poured in and took possession. In judging of the history of early Christianity in Britain it must always be remembered that the people who brought it in on the East coast were foreigners, who never amalgamated with the natives. Augustine was Italian, and for more than a century no native Britons were advanced to high places in the Church. Theodore of Tarsus, with the aid of Hadrian, the negro, organized the Church in England in the seventh century; Italians and other aliens held the high offices. The Augustine mission and their successors concentrated on the rulers, and through them forced their exotic religion on a stubborn and unwilling people. This is very clear in the reign of Canute, whose conversion was hardly two generations before the Norman Conquest; in his zeal for his new religion he tried to suppress heathenism by legal enactments.

No religion dies out with the dramatic suddenness claimed by the upholders of the Complete-Conversion theory. The constant influx of Pagans through several centuries more than counterbalanced the small number of immigrant Christians. The country must therefore have been Pagan with Christian rulers and a Christian aristocracy. A parallel case is that of Spain under the Moslems. There the rulers were of one religion, the people of another, the popular religion receiving continual reinforcements from abroad. In the case of Spain the popular religion organized by the civil power drove out the superimposed cult. In England, however, the final conquest was by the Normans, whose ruler was of the same religion as that of the king whom he defeated; but the Norman people, like the English, were largely of the Old Faith, and the Conquest made little difference to the relative position of the two religions. Therefore though the rulers professed Christianity the great mass of the people followed the old gods, and even in the highest offices of the Church the priests often served the heathen deities as well as the Christian God and practised Pagan rites. Thus in 1282 the priest of Inverkeithing led the fertility dance round the churchyard;[2] in 1303 the bishop of Coventry, like other members of his diocese, paid homage to a deity in the form of an animal;[3] in 1453, two years before the Rehabilitation of Joan of Arc, the Prior of Saint-Germain-en-Laye performed the same rites as the bishop of Coventry.[4] As late as 1613 de Lancre can say of the Basses Pyrénées, 'the greater part of the priests are witches',[5] while Madame Bourignon in 1661 records at Lille that 'no Assemblies were ever seen so numerous in the City as in these Sabbaths, where came People of all Qualities and Conditions, Young and Old, Rich and Poor, Noble and Ignoble, but especially all sorts of Monks and Nuns, Priests and Prelates'.[6] The political aspect of the organization is well exemplified in the trial of the North Berwick witches, when at the instance of their Grandmaster they attempted to kill James VI. Another example is found among the Elizabethan State Papers;[7] 'The names of the Confederates against Her Majesty who have diverse and sundry times conspired her life and do daily confederate against her Ould Birtles the great devel, Darnally the sorcerer, Maude Two-good enchantress, the ould witch of Ramsbury'.

William the Conqueror rendered waste and desolate nearly half of his new kingdom; the re-peopling of the wilderness seems to have been done in great measure by the descendants of the Neolithic and Bronze Age stock who were saved from massacre by the remoteness and inaccessibility of their dwellings. These were the places where the Old Religion flourished; and it was only by very slow degrees that even a small amount of outward conformity with Christianity could be established, and then only by means of compromises on the part of the Church; certain practices were permitted, certain images were retained, though often under different names.

The Reformation appears to have had the same effect on Great Britain as the Mahommedan conquest had on Egypt. The Moslems found Christianity established in the towns of the Nile Valley while a debased Paganism still existed among the agricultural population. The religion of Islam swept through the country like a flame, the converts being chiefly from the Pagans, not from the Christians. In Great Britain the appeal of the Reformation, like the appeal of the even more fanatical Islam, was to the Pagan population; but with this difference, that in England political conditions brought in the higher classes as well. It was then that the dividing line between Christianity and heathenism became more marked, for the Old Religion was gradually relegated to the lowest classes of the community and to those who lived in remote parts at a distance from any centre of civilization.

The records of the Middle Ages show that the ancient god was known in many parts of the country, but to the Christian recorder he was the enemy of the New Religion and was therefore equated with the Principle of Evil, in other words the Devil. This conception, that a god other than that of the recorder must be evil, is not confined to Christianity, or to the Middle Ages. Saint Paul, in the First Epistle to the Corinthians, expressed the same opinion when

Introduction

he wrote: 'The things which the Gentiles sacrifice, they sacrifice to devils and not to God. Ye cannot drink the cup of the Lord and the cup of devils; ye cannot be partakers of the Lord's table and the table of devils.' The author of the Book of Revelation is equally definite when he calls the magnificent altar of Zeus at Pergamos 'the throne of Satan', 'I know thy works and where thou dwellest, even where Satan's throne is'. In 1613 Sebastian Michaelis spoke with no uncertain voice, 'The Gods of the Turks and the Gods of the Gentiles are all Devils'. In India, Hindus, Mahommedans and Christians unite in calling the deities of the aboriginal tribes 'devils'. The gentle peaceable Yezidis of modern Mesopotamia, whose god is incarnate in a peacock or a black snake, are stigmatized as 'devil-worshippers' by their Moslem fellow-countrymen. As late as the nineteenth century Christian missionaries of every denomination, who went out to convert the heathen in any part of the world, were apt to speak of the people among whom they laboured as worshippers of devils, and many even believed that those to whom they preached were doomed to hell-fire unless they turned to the Christian God. The gods of the Pagans were often accredited with evil magical powers, which could be mysteriously communicated to the priests. Against such powers of hell the Christian missionaries felt themselves strengthened by the powers of heaven; and the belief that the devil had been defeated by the Archangel Michael backed by the whole power of the Almighty gave them courage in the contest.

The study of anthropology has changed much of this childish method of regarding the forms of religious belief which belong to another race or another country. To consider Islam, Buddhism, or Hinduism as the invention of the Evil One would be thought ridiculous at the present day, even the fetishes and the images of the more savage races are treated with respect as being sacred to their worshippers.

But though there is no difficulty in realizing the fact that 'heathen' religions exist outside Europe, there is still a strong

20

feeling among Christians that Christianity is so essentially European that no other religion could have remained after it was once introduced. The evidence, however, points to an entirely different conclusion. Until almost the time of the Norman Conquest the legal enactments show that though the rulers might be nominally Christian the people were openly heathen. It is possible that the Church's prohibition against representing the Crucifixion as a lamb on a cross was due to the desire to differentiate the Christian from the heathen god. The lamb, being a horned animal, was liable to be confounded with the horned deity of the Pagans.

The desolation of the country by the Conqueror would not increase the estimation of Christianity in the eyes of the unhappy population, and the Old Religion must have survived if only as a protest against the horrors inflicted by the worshipper of the new God. The number of times that the 'Devil' is said to have appeared in the reign of Rufus is very suggestive of this.

In the thirteenth century the Church opened its long-drawn-out conflict with Paganism in Europe by declaring 'witchcraft' to be a 'sect' and heretical. It was not till the fourteenth century that the two religions came to grips. The bishop of Coventry in 1303 escaped probably because he belonged to both faiths, but the next trial was fought out to the end. In 1324 the bishop of Ossory tried Dame Alice Kyteler in his ecclesiastical court for the crime of worshipping a deity other than the Christian God. The evidence proved the truth of the accusation, which the lady apparently did not deny, but she was of too high rank to be condemned and she escaped out of the bishop's hands. Not so her followers, who paid at the stake the penalty of differing from the Church. The next step was the investigation into the Old Religion at Berne, given to the world in Nider's *Formicarius*. Here again the Church could seize only the poorer members, those of high rank were too powerful to be sent to their deaths and went free.

The fifteenth century marks the first great victories of the

Church. Beginning with the trials in Lorraine in 1408 the Church moved triumphantly against Joan of Arc and her followers in 1431, against Gilles de Rais and his coven in 1440, against the witches of Brescia in 1457. Towards the end of the century the Christian power was so well established that the Church felt that the time had come for an organized attack, and in 1484 pope Innocent VIII published his Bull against 'witches'. All through the sixteenth and seventeenth centuries the battle raged. The Pagans fought a gallant, though losing, fight against a remorseless and unscrupulous enemy; every inch of the field was disputed. At first victory occasionally inclined to the Pagans, but the Christian policy of obtaining influence over the rulers and law-givers was irresistible. *Vae victis* was also the policy of the Christians, and we see the priests of the Papacy gloating over the thousands whom they had consigned to the flames while the ministers of the Reformed Churches hounded on the administrators of the law to condemn the 'devil-worshippers'. What can have been the feelings with which those unhappy victims regarded the vaunted God of Love, the Prince of Peace, whose votaries condemned them to torture and death? What wonder that they clung to their old faith, and died in agony unspeakable rather than deny their God.

The Horned God

'The God of the old religion becomes the Devil of the new.'

The earliest known representation of a deity is in the Caverne des Trois Frères in Ariège, and dates to the late Palaeolithic period (Plate 2). The figure is that of a man clothed in the skin of a stag and wearing on his head the antlers of a stag. The hide of the animal covers the whole of the man's body, the hands and feet are drawn as though seen through a transparent material; thus conveying to the spectator the information that the figure is a disguised human being. The face is bearded, the eyes large and round, but there is some doubt whether the artist intended to represent the man-animal with a mask or with the face uncovered.

The horned man is drawn on the upper part of the wall of the cave, below and around him are representations of animals painted in the masterly manner characteristic of the Palaeolithic artist. It seems evident from the relative position of all the figures that the man is dominant and that he is in the act of performing some ceremony in which the animals are concerned. The ceremony appears to consist of a dance with movements of the hands as well as the feet. It is worth noting that though the pictures of the animals are placed where they can easily be seen by the spectator the horned man can only be viewed from that part of the cavern which is most difficult of access. This fact suggests that a great degree of sanctity was attached to this representation, and that it was purposely placed where it was screened from the gaze of the vulgar.

The period when the figure was painted is so remote that it is not possible to make any conjectures as to its meaning except by the analogy of historical and modern instances. Such instances are, however, sufficiently numerous to render it fairly certain that the man represents the incarnate god, who, by performing the sacred dance, causes the increase of the kind of animal in the disguise of which he appears.

Though the stag-man is the most important of the horned figures of the Palaeolithic period, there are many smaller drawings of masked and horned men on small objects of bone and horn. These figures are usually represented with the horns of a goat or chamois, and are dancing singly or in groups. The most interesting example is on Plate 3, where the horned man is not only dancing but also accompanies himself on a kind of musical bow. The only Palaeolithic representation of a human figure found in England is the well-known engraving on bone of a man masked with a horse's head, which was discovered in the Pinhole Cave, Derbyshire.

The art of the Palaeolithic period came to a sudden and complete end before the Neolithic era; it was utterly wiped out in Europe, and seems to have had no influence on later periods. The Neolithic people have left few artistic remains; their human figures are almost invariably of women, and the masked man does not appear. But when the Bronze Age is reached the horned human-being is found again, and occurs first in the Near and Middle East, i.e. in Egypt, Mesopotamia and India. In the Near East the figures may be either male or female, and the horns are those of cattle, sheep or goats.[1] There are no stag antlers, possibly because the stag did not occur in those lands or was so uncommon as not to be of importance as a food animal.

Horned gods were common in Mesopotamia, both in Babylon and Assyria. The copper head found in one of the gold-tombs at Ur, is very early; possibly earlier than the first Egyptian dynasty. It is about half life-size, and the style and workmanship show an advanced stage of metal-working.

The eyes were originally inlaid with limestone or shell for the white of the eye, and lapis lazuli for the iris. The head wears two horns, a number which at a slightly later period would indicate that the wearer was an inferior deity; for, during many centuries, the position of a deity in the Babylonian pantheon was shown by the number of horns worn. The great gods and goddesses had seven horns, which is perhaps the reason that the divine Lamb in the Book of Revelation was said to have seven horns. The two-horned deities of Babylonia are so numerous that it is likely that they were originally the deities of the primitive inhabitants, who had to take a lower place when the great gods were introduced; these latter were given more horns than the godlings to show their superior position. The horns were a sign of divinity. When the King or High-priest appeared as the god Asshur with the Queen or High-priestess as his consort Ishtar, the appropriate number of horns was worn on the royal head-dresses, the royal pair being then regarded as the incarnate deities. When Alexander the Great raised himself above the kings of the earth and made himself a god, he wore horns in sign of his divinity, hence his name in the Koran, *Dhu'l Karnain* The Two-horned. In Egypt his horns were those of Amon, the supreme god.

Throughout the Bronze and Iron Ages horned deities are to be found in Egypt. The earliest example has a woman's face and the horns of a buffalo; this is on the slate-palette of Narmer,[2] who is usually identified with the first historic king of Egypt. It is worth noting that, with the exception of the god Mentu, the horns of cattle are worn by goddesses only, while the gods have the horns of sheep. The chief of the horned gods of Egypt was Amon, originally the local deity of Thebes, later the supreme god of the whole country. He is usually represented in human form wearing the curved horns of the Theban ram. Herodotus mentions that at the great annual festival at Thebes the figure of Amon was wrapped in a ram's skin, evidently in the same way that the dancing god of Ariège was wrapped. There were two types of sheep whose horns were the insignia of divinity; the Theban breed had curved horns, but the ordinary breed of ancient Egyptian sheep had twisted horizontal horns. The horizontal horns are those most commonly worn by Egyptian gods. One of the most important of these deities is Khnum, the god of the district round the First Cataract; he was a creator god and was represented as a human being with a sheep's head and horizontal horns. But the greatest of all the horned gods of Egypt was Osiris, who appears to have been the Pharaoh in his aspect as the incarnate god. The crown of Osiris, of which the horizontal horns were an important part, was also the crown of the monarch, indicating to all who understood the symbolism that the king as god was the giver of all fertility.

In the accounts of the divine birth of the Egyptian Kings, the future father of the divine child, the Pharaoh, visits the queen as the god Amon wearing all the insignia of divinity including the horns. In this connection it should also be noted that down to the latest period of pharaonic history the divine father was always the horned Amon.

There are two other links between Egypt and the dancing god of Ariège. On a slate palette, which is dated to the period just before the beginning of Egyptian history, there is represented a man with the head and tail of a jackal;[3] as in the Ariège example the body, hands and feet are human; he plays on a flute, and like the Palaeolithic god he is in the midst of animals. The other link is in the ceremonial dress of the Pharaoh, who on great occasions wore a bull's tail attached to his girdle. The *sed-heb* or Tail-festival, when the king was invested with the tail, was one of the most important of the royal ceremonies. A sacred dance, performed by the Pharaoh wearing the bull's tail, is often represented as taking place in a temple before Min, the god of human generation. The worship of horned gods continued in Egypt until Christian times, especially in connection with the horned goddess Isis.

The Indian figures of the Horned God, found at Mohenjo-Daro, are of the earliest Bronze Age. There are many examples, and in every case it is clear that a human being is represented, either masked or horned. Sometimes the figure has a human body with a bull's head, sometimes the head and body are covered with a hairy skin, probably indicating a bull's hide. The most remarkable is that of a man with bull's horns on his head, sitting cross-legged, and like the Ariège figure surrounded with animals (Plate 4*a*). This representation was regarded in historic times as a form of Shiva and is called Pasupati, 'Lord of animals'. When in relief sculpture Pasupati is three-faced, as here; but in figures in the round he has four faces. Such a representation is a naïve attempt to show the all-seeing god, and is found in Europe in the four-faced Janus. It is still uncertain whether the four-faced form arose independently in India and Europe, or whether one is the prototype of the other; if the latter, the Indian appears to be the earlier.

Though it is not possible to give an exact date to the early legends of the Aegean, it is evident that there also the Horned God flourished throughout the Bronze and Iron Ages.

The best known, on account of the dramatic legends attached to his cult, was the Minoan bull, the Minotaur, of Crete. He was in human form with a bull's head and horns, and was worshipped with sacred dances and human sacrifices. He was said to be the offspring of a foreign 'bull' and the Cretan queen, who at the marriage appeared in the guise of a cow, in other words, she was robed and masked as an animal like the dancing god of Ariège. The representations of the combat between Theseus and the Minotaur show the latter as entirely human, with a bull's mask (Plate 5*a*). Theseus is sometimes represented with the flowing locks of the Cretan athlete; this suggests that the slaying may have been a Cretan custom, the man representing the Minotaur being killed in a battle in which, masked as he was, he could be no match for his antagonist. Frazer has pointed out that Minos went to Zeus every nine years, and has suggested that this was a euphemism for the sacrifice of each ruler at the end of that term of years. In the Theseus legend the interval of time was seven years, but the rest of the story so closely resembles other accounts of the sacrifice by combat that it cannot be disregarded; Theseus did not put an end to the custom, he merely relieved Athens from sending the yearly victims, who, like the children stolen by the fairies, had to 'pay the teind to hell' with their lives.

The sanctity of the ram in the Aegean in the early Bronze Age is shown in the legend of Helle and Phrixos. They were the children of the family who were set apart as victims when human sacrifice was required. The sacrifice of Helle was consummated by drowning, but Phrixos escaped by means of the divine animal, which he afterwards sacrificed, possibly as a substitute for himself. The story of Jason's expedition suggests that the fleece had a divine connotation, and that its value was greatly in excess of the intrinsic worth of the gold.

Of the horned gods of the mainland of Greece, Pan is the best known to the modern world, yet he is but one among many horned deities of the eastern Mediterranean (Plate 5*b*). His universality is shown by his name, which points to a time when he was the only deity in his own locality. All representations of him are necessarily late, after the fifth century B.C.; but even in the earliest forms his characteristics are the same, the long narrow face, the pointed beard, the small horns, and the goat's legs. Scenes of his worship show him followed by a dancing procession of satyrs and nymphs, while he plays on the pipes which bear his name. His appearance should be compared with the little dancing god of the Palaeolithic people (Plate 3), and also with the figure of Robin Goodfellow (Plate 11). Though our knowledge of him dates only to the late Iron Age, his worship is obviously of high antiquity, and he appears to be indigenous in Greece.

Another horned god of Greece was Bull Dionysos, who, like the Minotaur of Crete, was slain. Dionysos was said to have been brought into Greece from the north; his cult would therefore be a foreign worship, which fact shows that outside Greece, in the countries which have no written record, the belief in a horned deity prevailed in the Iron Age and probably even earlier.

A few rock carvings in Scandinavia show that the horned god was known there also in the Bronze Age. It was only when Rome started on her career of conquest that any written record was made of the gods of western Europe, and those records prove that a horned deity, whom the Romans called Cernunnos, was one of the greatest gods, perhaps even the supreme deity, of Gaul. The name given to him by the Romans means simply The Horned. In the north of Gaul his importance is shown on the altar found under the cathedral of Notre Dame at Paris. The date of the altar is well within the Christian era; on three sides are figures of minor gods represented as small beings, on the fourth side is the head of Cernunnos (Plate 6a), which is of huge proportions compared with the other figures. He has a man's head, and like the Ariège figure he wears stag's antlers, which are further decorated with rings; these may be hoops of withy or bronze currency-rings. Like his Palaeolithic prototype he is bearded. This altar shows that, in accordance with Roman artistic ideas, the divine man was not masked, he wears the horns and their appendages fixed on his head. The altar appears to have been dedicated in a temple so sacred that the site was re-used for the principal temple of the new faith. Cernunnos is recorded in writing and in sculpture in the south of Gaul, in that very part where the Palaeolithic painting of him still survives. It is highly improbable that the cult of the Horned God should have died out in south-western Europe in Neolithic times and have remained unknown through the Bronze and Iron Ages, only to be revived before the arrival of the Romans. It is more logical to suppose that the worship continued through the unrecorded centuries, and lasted on as one of the principal Gaulish cults till within the Christian era. Such a cult must have had a strong hold on the worshippers, and among the illiterate, and in the less accessible parts of the country it would linger for many centuries after a new religion had been accepted elsewhere.

The Horned God

In considering the evidence from Britain the proximity of Gaul to this country and the constant flux of peoples from one shore to the other, must be taken into account. What is true of Gaul is true of Britain, some allowance being made for the differences caused by the effect of another climate on temperament and on conditions of life.

Our chief knowledge of the horned god in the British Isles comes from ecclesiastical and judicial records. As these were made exclusively by Christians, generally priests, the religious bias is always very marked. The worshippers themselves were illiterate and have left no records of their beliefs except in a few survivals here and there. The earliest record of the masked and horned man in England is in the *Liber Poenitentialis*[4] of Theodore, who was Archbishop of Canterbury from 668 to 690, and ruled the Church in England with the assistance of Hadrian the negro. This was a time when—if we are to believe the ecclesiastical chroniclers—England was practically Christianized, yet Theodore fulminates against anyone who 'goes about as a stag or a bull; that is, making himself into a wild animal and dressing in the skin of a herd animal, and putting on the heads of beasts; those who in such wise transform themselves into the appearance of a wild animal, penance for three years because this is devilish'. Three centuries later King Edgar[5] found that the Old Religion was more common than the official faith, and he urges that 'every Christian should zealously accustom his children to Christianity.'

The great influx of heathen Norsemen, under Sweyn and Canute into England and under Rollo into France, must have been a terrible blow to Christianity in western Europe, in spite of the so-called conversion of the rulers. Though the New Religion steadily gained ground, the Old Religion regained many 'converts', and more than one ruler held firmly to the faith of his fathers. This was markedly the case among the East Saxons, the most powerful kingdom in the seventh and eighth centuries. The East Saxon kings must have been peculiarly irritating to the Christian missionaries, for the rise and fall of the two religions alternately is instructive. In 616 Sebert, the Christian king, died and was succeeded by his three sons who maintained the Old Religion and drove out the Christians. The New Religion apparently gained ground later, for in 654 their successor was 'converted'. Ten years after, in 664, King Sighere and the greater number of his people threw off Christianity and returned to the ancient faith. Even when the king was not averse to Christianity he was apt to act in a disconcerting manner by trying to serve two masters. Thus, according to Bede, King Redwald had 'in the same temple an altar to sacrifice to Christ, and another smaller one to offer victims to devils'. At the end of the ninth century the whole of the powerful kingdom of Mercia was under the sway of the heathen Danes; and Penda, one of the greatest of the Mercian rulers, refused to change his religion and died, as he had lived, a devout Pagan.

The same difficulties occurred elsewhere. In Normandy Rollo, after his conversion, gave great gifts to Christian churches, but at the same time sacrificed his Christian captives to his old gods. Scandinavia, always in touch with Great Britain (Norway held the Hebrides till 1263), successfully resisted Christianity till the eleventh century. Sweyn, the son of Harold Bluetooth, was baptized in infancy, but when he became a man he reverted to the old faith and waged a religious war against his Christian father; and as late as the end of the thirteenth century a Norwegian king was known as 'the Priest-hater'.

There is no doubt that the records are incomplete and that if all the instances of renunciation of Christianity had been as carefully recorded as the conversions it would be seen that the rulers of western Europe were not Christian except in name for many centuries after the arrival of the missionaries. Until the Norman Conquest the Christianity of England was the very thinnest veneer over an underlying Paganism; the previous centuries of Christian archbishops and bishops had not succeeded in doing more than wrest an outward conformity from the rulers and chiefs, while the people and many of the so-called Christian priests remained in unabated heathenism.

That the worshippers regarded the so-called 'Devil' as truly God is clearly seen in the evidence even when recorded by their fanatical enemies. In more than one case it is remarked that the witch 'refused to call him the Devil', and in many instances the accused explicitly called him god. The following instances are not exhaustive, they cover a century and are taken from the actual trials as well as from the generalizations of those writers who heard the evidence at first-hand and had themselves tried many cases. Danaeus[6] was such an author, he wrote in 1575 that the 'witches acknowledge the Devil for their god, call upon him, pray to him, and trust in him', and that when they go to the Sabbath 'they repeat the oath which they have given unto him in acknowledging him to be their God'. Of the Aberdeen witches, tried in 1596,[7] Agnes Wobster was accused of having dealings with 'Satan whom thou callest thy God'; Marion Grant confessed that Christsonday was the name of the Divine Personage, 'Christsonday bade thee call him Lord, and caused thee to worship him on thy knees as thy Lord'. Boguet,[8] the Inquisitor, who records with unction that he tried and executed many witches in France in 1608, states that 'the witches, before taking their repast, bless the table, but with words full of blasphemy, making Beelzebub the author and protector of all things'. De Lancre,[9] the Inquisitor in the Pays de Labourd (Basses Pyrénées), wrote in 1613 that there was 'a great Devil, who is the master of all, whom they all adore'; he also recorded the evidence of one of his victims,[10] 'the Devil made them believe that he was the true God', and he gives as a general statement[11] 'our witches for the most part hold these Demons as Gods'. In Orleans in 1614[25] 'they say to the Devil, we recognize you as our Master, our God, our Creator'. At Edmonton in 1621 Elizabeth Sawyer[12] confessed that 'he charged me to pray no more to Jesus Christ, but to him the Devil.' In Lancashire in 1633 Margaret Johnson[13] 'met a spirit or devil in

4a. A HORNED GOD (PASUPATI)

From Mohenjo-Daro

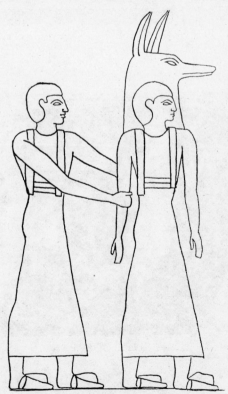

4b. EGYPTIAN PRIEST WEARING
JACKAL MASK

5a. THESEUS SLAYING THE MINOTAUR

5b. THE GOD PAN

a suit of black tied about with silk points', he instructed her to call him Mamilion, 'and in all her talk and conference she called the said Mamilion her god'. Gaule, making a general statement about witch-beliefs and practices in 1646,[14] says that the witches 'promise to take him for their God, worship, invoke, obey him'. Of the Essex and Suffolk witches, whose trials made such a stir in 1646,[15] Rebecca West 'confessed that her mother prayed constantly (and as the world thought, very seriously) but she said it was to the Devil, using these words, *Oh my God, my God,* meaning him and not the Lord'. Ellen Greenleife also 'confessed that when she prayed she prayed to the Devil and not to God'. Widow Coman[16] 'did acknowledge that she had made an agreement with him and that he was her Master and sat at the right hand of God'. The author of the *Pleasant Treatise of Witches,* whose violent hatred towards those unhappy beings is only equalled in bitterness by that of the Inquisitors, states in 1673 that at the Sabbath 'they make their accustomed homage, Adoring and Proclaiming him their Lord'. In the same year at Newcastle-on-Tyne[17] Ann Armstrong testified that she had heard Ann Baites 'calling him sometimes her protector, and other sometimes her blessed saviour'; and that 'he was their protector, which they called their God'. The Salem witch, Mary Osgood, in 1692, said [18] that 'the Devil told her he was her God, and that she should serve and worship him'.

Such a mass of evidence shows that till the end of the seventeenth century the Old Religion still counted large numbers of members. The issue has been confused, perhaps purposely, by the use of the word *Devil* in its Christian connotation, for the name of the God, and by stigmatizing the worshippers as witches. The consequence is that the pagan people are now regarded as having worshipped the Principle of Evil, though in reality they were merely following the cult of a non-Christian Deity.

The first recorded instance of the continuance of the worship of the Horned God in Britain is in 1303, when the Bishop of Coventry was accused before the Pope of doing homage to the Devil in the form of a sheep.[19] The fact that a man in so high a position as a bishop could be accused of practising the Old Religion shows that the cult of the Horned God was far from being dead, and that it was in all probability still the chief worship of the bulk of the people. It should be also noticed that this is one of the first British records in which the old God is called the Devil by the Christian writers of the Middle Ages.

It is possible that the bishop's high position in the Christian hierarchy saved him from punishment, for in the case also of the Lady Alice Kyteler in 1324 her rank as a noble saved her when she was tried before the bishop of Ossory for her heathen practices.[20] The bishop, however, had sufficient evidence to prove his case and sufficient power to burn the lady's poorer co-religionists, though not herself.

Herne the Hunter, with horns on his head, was seen in Windsor Forest by the Earl of Surrey in the reign of Henry VIII, and after that period it was a favourite accusation against all political enemies that they were in league with 'the foul fiend' who appeared to them in human form horned like a bull or a stag. Thus John Knox was said to have held converse with the devil in the Cathedral churchyard at St. Andrews.[21] There is still extant a record that Cromwell made a pact for seven years with the Devil on the night before the battle of Worcester, and he not only won an overwhelming victory but died that very day seven years later in the middle of the worst thunderstorm within human memory; which was proof positive of the truth of the story in the minds of the Royalists.[22] On the other hand the Royalists of Scotland were believed to have sold themselves to the Evil One. The bishops were said to be cloven-footed and to cast no shadows, and those justices of the peace appointed to try the political prisoners were seen often talking in a friendly way with the Devil.[23]

This uninterrupted record of belief in a horned deity shows that underlying the official religion of the rulers there still remained the ancient cult with all its rites almost untouched.

The Horned God

In the depositions of the witches at the trials the Horned God is very prominent at the great assemblies. The horns and animal disguise were his 'grand array', but in his ordinary intercourse with his flock the Incarnate God appeared in the dress of the period. Here again the congregation would see no difference between their own and the Christian priest, who also wore special vestments when performing religious ceremonies. This alteration of costume is specially noted by de Lancre,[24] 'It is always observable that at any time when he is about to receive anyone to make a pact with him, he presents himself always as a man, in order not to scare or terrify them; for to make a compact openly with a goat smacks more of the beast than of a reasonable creature. But the compact being made, when he receives anyone for adoration he usually represents himself as a goat.'

The evidence that the Devil appeared as a man to a possible convert is found continually, and it is very obvious that he was actually a human being. Thus in 1678[25] the Devil appeared as a man to Mr. Williamson, a school-master at Coupar; he gave Mr. Williamson a dinner, and meeting him again in London treated him again. In 1682[26] Susanna Edwards, a Devonshire witch, stated that 'about two years ago she did meet with a gentleman in a field called the Parsonage Close in the town of Biddiford. And saith that his apparel was all black. Upon which she did hope to have a piece of money of him. Whereupon the gentleman drawing near unto this examinant, she did make a curchy or courtesy unto him, as she did use to do to gentlemen. Being demanded what and who the gentleman she spoke of was, the said examinant answered and said, That it was the Devil.' These are only two instances out of very many.

The forms in which the disguised god appeared were bull, cat, dog, goat, horse, sheep, and stag. It is noteworthy that the goat and sheep do not occur in Great Britain except in the case of the Norman Bishop of Coventry; they belong almost entirely to France and Germany. In England, Scotland, and the south of France the usual animal disguise was the bull or the stag; but nowhere is there a record of the head of the religion appearing as an ass, or a hare, though the hare was the most common transformation of the witches; in late times, in France and Germany he is occasionally a pig. In Guernsey there is a record of a peculiar disguise, when in 1617 Isabel Becquet[27] went to the Sabbath at Rocquaine Castle and there saw the Devil in the form of a dog with two great horns sticking up, and 'with one of his paws (which seemed to her like hands) took her by the hand: and calling her by her name told her that she was welcome.'

In all cases of the Devil as an animal the evidence of the witches shows that it was undoubtedly a disguise. Besides the dog with horns and human hands mentioned above, there are numerous other instances. At Angers[28] in 1593, the 'Black Man' transformed himself first into a goat and then into a young bull; in Guernsey[29] in 1563 he was a large black cat who led the dance; in 1616 at Brécy[30] he was a black dog who stood on his hind-legs and preached; at Poictiers in 1574[21] he was a goat who talked like a person; at Avignon[32] in 1581, when he mounted on an altar to be adored 'he instantly turns himself into the form of a great black goat, although on all other occasions he useth to appear in the shape of a man.' In Auldearne[33] in 1662 'sometimes he would be like a stirk, a bull, a deer, a roe, or a dog.'

It is only necessary to look at the figure of the dancing god of Ariège (Plate 2) to see that in all the medieval cases we are dealing with a man in some kind of disguise. The description given by Agnes Sampson, one of the leaders of the North Berwick witches, of the so-called Devil of her coven would apply equally well to the Ariège figure. 'His face was terrible, his nose like the beak of an eagle, great burning eyes, his hands and legs were hairy, with claws upon his hands, and feet like the griffin.'[34] Yet there is probably not less than eight thousand years between the painting and the recorded description. Again in a scene of worship on an Egyptian papyrus of the XXIInd dynasty, about the tenth century B.C., a woman is depicted in the act of praying to

her god (Plate 7). But the description given by Isobel Gowdie in 1662 of a ceremony performed by herself and her
coven would apply to the scene on the papyrus. 'When we
had learned all these words from the Devil, we all fell down
upon our knees, with our hair down over our shoulders and
eyes, and our hands lifted up, and our eyes steadfastly fixed
upon the Devil, and said the foresaid words thrice over to
the Devil.'[35] The flowing hair and the uplifted hands and
eyes, as well as the horned god, are alike in both Egypt and
Scotland. No one would hesitate to say that the Egyptian
lady was engaged in the worship of her god, who was symbolized to her in the figure of a goat, yet most people of the
present day are horrified to think that less than three centuries ago a similar worship of a 'heathen' god was still
practised in the British Isles.

The ritual masking of the Incarnate God or his priest is
found in many places after the Palaeolithic period. Besides
the dancing god there are the little masked and horned
figures. I have already called attention to these in their geographical and chronological order, but it is important to note
that figures of maskers and the masks themselves still survive. On the so-called Hunting Palette of predynastic Egypt[36]
the figure of a man disguised as a jackal and playing on a
flute suggests the black-dog disguise of the European Devil.
A jackal mask belonging to the XXVIth dynasty, about the
seventh century B.C., is made of pottery and is intended to
be worn over the head (Plate 8a). The method of wearing
it is shown in the procession of priests at Denderah, where
the masked priest has to be led by one of his fellows
(Plate 4b). This jackal-mask should be compared with the
'Dorset Ooser' (Plate 8b), which was stolen from its
Dorsetshire owners within the last thirty years. The Ooser
was of painted wood, and, like the Egyptian example, was
worn over the head, the wearer being at the same time
wrapped in an oxskin. The combination of the horned mask
and the animal's skin show too close a resemblance to the
Palaeolithic prototype to be accidental. In the Ooser we have

the last remains of that most ancient of all recorded religions, the worship of the Horned God.

The name of the great Pagan deity varied according to the country in which the cult was followed. In the Near East the names were recorded from very early times; the name of the Indian deity cannot yet be read, but the traditional name still survives; in Greece and in Crete the record is later than in Egypt and Babylonia. In western Europe, however, it was not till the Roman domination that any written records were made; therefore it is only by tradition and an occasional Roman inscription that the names of the horned god are known to us. The great Gaulish god was called by the Romans Cernunnos, which in English parlance was Herne, or more colloquially 'Old Hornie'.In northern Europe the ancient Neck or Nick, meaning a spirit, had such hold on the affections of the people that the Church was forced to accept him, and he was canonized as Saint Nicholas, who in Cornwall still retains his horns. Our Puck is the Welsh *Boucca*, which derives either directly from the Slavic *Bog* 'God' or from the same root. The word Bog is a good example of the fall of the High God to a lower estate, for it becomes our own Bogey and the Scotch Bogle, both being diminutives of the original word connoting a small and therefore evil god.

Many of the names of the Devils appear to be diminutives. Thus among the group of Alsatian witches tried between 1585 and 1630,[37] the names for the Devil (i.e. the God) were Hämmerlin, Peterlin, and Kochlöffel. The first of these may mean a yellow-hammer, always regarded as the Devil's bird, but as the name is also given as Hammer it is suggestive of a diminutive of an epithet of Thor; Peterlin may be the Christianized form of a local deity; for Kochlöffel (Cooking-spoon) I can offer no explanation except that it may be a mispronunciation of a traditional name. According to de Lancre the name of the Basque god was Jauna or Janicot.[38] The latter he regarded as a diminutive and says that it means 'petit Jean', and was applied by the witches of the Basses

Pyrénées to Christ; a man-witch at Orleans also spoke of the host as '*un beau Janicot*'.[39] It may however not be a diminutive, but a form of Jauna with the ending *Cot* 'God', as in the Northern Irmincot. In modern times the god, who has now degenerated into a sprite, is known by the Basques as Basa-Jaun, the equivalent of *Homme de Bouc*, Goat-man,[40] which brings the whole of the early religion of the Basques into connection with the Horned God. De Lancre notes that the witches, when 'in the hands of Justice' used the name Barrabam[41] to signify either their own or the Christian God, Barrabon[42] being also the name of a witch-god in Belgium.

A peculiar name, which occurs both in Great Britain and France is Simon; it was used for either the Grandmaster or for the familiars which were also called *devils*. It is possibly a diminutive like the Mamilion of Layamon's *Brut* (ll. 16790–5), or the Amaimon and Barbason of which Falstaff says, 'they are devil's additions, the name of fiends.' But there is another possible explanation. The early Christian Fathers refer to a statue to Simon set up in Rome in the reign of Claudius by the Roman people. The base of this statue has been found, and on it is a dedication to the ancient Sabine god, Semo Sancus. This important deity was the god of fertility as his name, Semo, implies; and as such the name might well have spread to Gaul and Britain with the Roman conquerors. Later, when Christianity was brought to England by foreign missionaries, the tonsure of the British Christian priesthood was stigmatized by the Augustinians as 'the tonsure of Simon Magus'. That the Biblical Simon Magus ever reached Britain is excessively unlikely, but the tonsure of priests was a heathen custom before it was adopted by Christianity, and the name given to the local tonsure in England is suggestive of the name of a heathen god.

The Aberdeen witches, tried in 1597,[43] called their Grandmaster 'Christsonday'. Andro Man confessed 'that Christsonday came to him in the likeness of a fair angel and clad in white clothes, and said that he was an angel, and that he should put his trust in him and call him Lord and King.'

And again, 'The Devil thy master, whom thou callest Christsonday and supposest to be an angel and God's god-son—albeit he has a thraw by God and sways to the Queen of Elfin—is raised by speaking the word *Benedicite* and is laid by speaking the word *Maikpeblis*. Suchlike thou affirmest that the Queen of Elfin has a grip of all the craft, but Christsonday is the goodman and has all power under God.' I suggest that the name Christsonday is a confusion of Christus Filius Dei, i.e. Son Dei, Dei being considered as a personal name by the ignorant worshippers. In the same way the Devil of Dame Alice Kyteler was called in the Latin record sometimes Robin Artisson, sometimes Robinus Filius Artis. The magical word Maikpeblis is probably, like Kochlöffel, a confused rendering of a traditional name.

The name of the god in Guernsey was Hou. This is clearly indicated by the version of the witch song or hymn quoted by Bodin in 1616,[44] where his 'diable' is the equivalent of the Guernsey Hou. Bodin's version is, '*Har, har, diable, diable, saute ici, saute là, joue ici, joue là*'; the Guernsey version runs, '*Har, har, Hou, Hou, danse ici, danse là, joue ici, joue là*'. The names of many of the smaller islands of the Channel Island group are compounded with the name of this obscure half-forgotten deity; Li-hou, Jet-hou, Brecq-hou, are instances. It is possible that the Welsh god, Hu Gadarn, Hu the Mighty, may be connected with the Guernsey deity. The name does not occur till the fifteenth century when it appears in a hymn, in which he is plainly called god. In view of the fact that the name is that of a 'devil' and that it is compounded with other elements in place-names, it seems not improbable that the god of the Old Religion survived in Wales where the Christian Church did not persecute. It is an interesting suggestion that the Har in the witch song is the same as the cry of Haro used in Guernsey as a cry for help against injustice.

The most interesting of all the names for the god is Robin, which when given to Puck is Robin Goodfellow. It is so common a term for the 'Devil' as to be almost a generic name for him, 'Some Robin the Divell, or I wot not what spirit of the Ayre'.[45] Dame Alice Kyteler called her god, Robin Artisson, and the Somerset witches[46] cried out 'Robin' when summoning their Grandmaster to a meeting, or even when about to make a private incantation; in the latter case they also added the words, 'O Satan, give me my purpose', and then proceeded to divine by the animal which appeared.

A fact, noted by many writers and still unexplained, is the connection between Robin Goodfellow and Robin Hood. Grimm remarks on it but gives no reason for his opinion, though the evidence shows that the connection is there. The cult of Robin Hood was widespread both geographically and in time, which suggests that he was more than a local hero in the places where his legend occurs. In Scotland as well as England Robin Hood was well known, and he belonged essentially to the people, not to the nobles. He was always accompanied by a band of twelve companions, very suggestive of a Grandmaster and his coven. One of those companions was Little John, a name which may be compared with the Basque Janicot. Robin Hood and his band were a constituent part of the May-day ceremonies, they had special dances and always wore the fairies' colour, green. He was so intimately connected with the May-day rites that even as early as 1580 Edmund Assheton[47] wrote to William ffarington about suppressing 'Robyn Hoode and the May games as being Lewde sportes, tending to no other end but to stir up our frail natures to wantonness.' In all the stories and traditions of Robin Hood his animosity to the Church is invariably emphasized, an abbot or prior was regarded as his legitimate prey. In one of the oldest Ballads of this popular hero, there is a description of how he went to be let blood by his cousin the prioress of a convent of nuns; she treacherously left the wound unbound and he bled to death. Part of the account shows, however, that his death was expected, for his route to the priory was lined with people, mourning and lamenting for his approaching death. The strong resemblance to the death-processions of Joan of Arc

and Gilles de Rais cannot be overlooked, the weeping praying populace are alike in all three cases.

If then there were more than one Robin Hood at the same
time in different parts of the country his ubiquity is explained; the name would then mean *Robin with a Hood*, and
would be the generic appellation of the god. In Chapter II
I have called attention to the great importance of the head-
covering among the fairy folk, and in many of the witch-
trials the 'Devil' is described as wearing a hood. The most
celebrated historical Robin Hood was the Earl of Huntingdon
in the reign of Richard I, who being himself a Plantagenet
belonged by race to the Old Religion. I have pointed out in
my *Witch Cult in Western Europe* that more than one Devil
can be identified, but in the earlier times the identification
becomes increasingly difficult as the ecclesiastical writers do
not record all the facts. It seems possible that the companions
of Robin Hood as the Incarnate God also bore special names,
for in the fifteenth century there is a pardon to a chaplain
which is so worded as to suggest this possibility. 'Pardon to
Robert Stafford, late of Lyndefeld, co. Sussex, chaplain, *alias*
Frere Tuk, for not appearing before the King to answer
Richard Wakehurst touching a plea of trespass.'[48]

The continuity of the Pagan religion through the medieval
period cannot be gainsaid when it is found surviving to the
present day. I quote from an article by the Rev. John Ray-
mond Crosby, D.D., D.C.L., Ph.D., in *The Living Church*
for 2 March 1929, which states that the rites are still to be
found in Pennsylvania and are practised by people who have
been in America for five generations. The Witch 'lives alone,
with the traditional black cat, in a small house filled with
herbs, charms and the implements of her profession. Her
compatriots have a firm conviction that she, together with
her ancestors for untold generations, entered into a definite
compact with the Devil who in his proper person is the father
of all the children of the family. Certain other members of
the sect, the Elect Ones, are permeated with the Spirit of
Good, and are regarded as incarnations of the Divine

Essence. It is the general belief that the witches hold regular gatherings for the practice of magical rites and the worship of the Evil Principle. They are reported to assume the form of animals, generally black, and to be restored to their original shapes at the rising of the sun. These meetings are illuminated by candles made of human fat, which renders the celebration invisible to all except the initiated.'

The most interesting modern survival of the Horned God occurs at the Puck Fair of Killorglin, co. Kerry. Though much of the ancient ritual is now irretrievably lost, enough remains to show the origin of the ceremonies.

The original date was Lammastide, i.e. the 1st of August, the date of one of the four Great Sabbaths of the Old Religion. The change of date to the 11th or 12th of August is due to the alteration in the calendar in 1752; by Old Style the present date would still be Lammastide. This was a well-known change of date, which affected many ancient customs and upset much weather lore. The frequenters of the Fair were probably reconciled to the change by the fact that the date now falls between Dublin Horse Show and Tramore Races, and they can therefore attend all three events.

Formerly the Fair was the time for family reunions, like the Sabbaths of the so-called 'witches', and like the modern Christmas. The Fair, however, is merely an adjunct to the real reason of the assembly. It is held outside the little town, and has all the usual and traditional methods of increasing enjoyment, merry-go-rounds, swings, booths for the sale of trifles, and refreshment bars. It is not an integral part of the festival, but is an addition to increase the general rejoicing and enjoyment. It is possible that some sort of fair accompanied the Great Sabbaths, for in 1609 de Lancre says: "Le sabbat est comme une foire de marchands."[49]

The Puck, after whom the Fair is called, is a male goat. This is a half-wild animal, living on the hills, and is caught for the sole purpose of presiding at the festival. Originally the privilege of providing the goat for the ceremony was vested in one family, though in recent years this has not always been the case.

The first day of the Fair is called Gathering Day. Crowds surge to and fro through the streets of the town and the alleys of the Fair, drinking and making merry. The Market Square is the centre of attraction at all times. Late in the afternoon but before sunset (5.30 p.m.) the Procession of the Goat begins. This consists of a Pipe-band, followed by a lorry, on which is the Puck-goat securely roped to a small platform. The Puck is decorated with wreaths round his neck, and is attended by four young boys dressed in green (Plate 16*a*). After parading round the town for an hour the band and the lorry return to the Square, where a light scaffolding, 35 feet high, has been erected. A little girl, dressed as a queen with a crown on her head, crowns the goat with a tinsel crown and casts a wreath of flowers round his neck (Plate 16*b*). Then the goat, still securely lashed to its platform, is hoisted with ropes and pulleys to the top of the scaffolding, where it remains till the close of the Fair. When the goat has reached its elevated position, a man proclaims through a megaphone, "The Puck King of Ireland". At all other times the goat is referred to as "The Puck King of the Fair". Food of the kind beloved of goats is hoisted up at intervals, so that the animal is overfed during his captivity.

The second day sees the festival at its height. The scenes, though now modified to drunkenness only, show that in early times this was one of those orgiastic festivals so common in primitive cults.

The third day is Scattering Day. The goat is lowered and set free, only to be caught again, if possible, to be the Puck King in the following year.

As I have already shown (p. 38), the name Puck is a derivative from the Slavonic word Bog, which means God. It seems clear, then, that this ceremony of the Puck King of Ireland is a survival of the worship of the Divine King, the Incarnate God, with an animal as the substitute for the man. I suggest that part of the original ceremony was the deification and crowning of a new King, with the worship and offerings made to him, and that the feasting and other rites practised at that time were emblematic of his power as the Giver of food and of all other forms of fertility. The boys in green and the crowned queen suggest a fairy, i.e. neolithic, origin; but it is now impossible to say whether their size is intended to suggest the Little People, or whether the fact of their being children was emblematic of the Puck King's power as the Giver of fertility.

As there is no trace of any killing of the animal it is clear that this ceremony is not the survival of the sacrifice of the Divine Man. It remains at present the only known survival of the deification and crowning of a king.

II

The Worshippers

'*In the hinder end of harvest, on All Hallow E'en,*
  When the Good Neighbours do ride, if I rede right,
Some buckled on a bune-wand, and some on a bean,
  Aye trottand in troops from the twilight;
Some saddled on a she-ape, all graithed into green,
  Some hobland on a hemp-stalk, hovand to the height,
The King of Pharie and his court, with the Elf-queen,
  With many elfish incubus was ridand that night.'
                                        MONTGOMERIE (1515)

Though to the modern reader, who has been brought up on the fairy tales of the present day, any connection between witches and fairies appears far-fetched and preposterous, yet in order to understand the one it is essential to take the other into account. Even when regarded superficially the likeness between the two is apparent. In stories of the baptism of a royal child the bad fairy, whether naturally malevolent or merely temporarily offended, gives evil gifts or enchants the unfortunate infant, and is thus indistinguishable from the witch. The traditional costume of the fairy godmother is precisely similar to that of the witch, both women carry sticks—a wand or a crutch—with which they perform magic, both can turn human beings into animals, both can appear or disappear at will. In short, the real difference is that the one is a dainty old lady and the other is a dirty old woman.

If then the fairy godmother and the witch are so closely identical, the question of fairies becomes important. The real difficulty in understanding the matter at the present day is due to the iron-bound prejudice of the modern reader in favour of the tiny elf, the 'two-inch men', the little creatures who can 'creep into an acorn-cup' or ride on a butterfly. These fragile little things have gossamer wings, they float on a moonbeam, they play among the blossoms, they dance in the flowery meadows. Everything about them is in miniature, and it would hardly be an alarming experience for a mortal to meet a fairy, a creature he could crush between his finger and thumb. Why then were our ancestors so afraid of fairies? The horror and fear of them is seen in all the records of the trials in which a witch is accused of visiting the fairy-folk.

This horror is expressed in numerous popular rhymes and in popular tales as well as by the poets. A charm to be said at night runs as follows:

> *Saint Francis and Saint Benedight,*
> *Bless this house from wicked wight,*
> *From the nightmare and the goblin*
> *That is hight Goodfellow Robin;*
> *Keep it from all evil spirits,*
> *Fairies, weasels, rats, and ferrets;*
> *From curfew time*
> *To the next prime.*

As late as 1600 Fairfax in his translation of Tasso could bracket the fairies with furies and ghosts:

> *The shriking gobblings each where howling flew,*
> *The Furies roare, the ghosts and Fairies yell.*

The Swedish bishop, Olaus Magnus, writing in 1555, says that 'there were Nightwalkers that used to enclose and strangely to disturb the field-keepers looking to their charge, with prodigious and wonderful sights of divers kinds, the inhabitants thereabouts call this nightly sport of Monsters, the Elves dance'[1] (Plate 14a).

In the stories of fairies it is not uncommon to find that the mortal is frightened at meeting the Little People: 'She was not a little terrified at seeing, though it was midday, some of the old elves of the blue petticoat.'[2] But the most alarming of all the fairies was Robin Goodfellow until Shakespeare made him subordinate to Oberon. The evidence shows that Robin was not a fairy but the god of the Little People, as I have already noted in the previous chapter. According to Keightley his names are Puck, Robin Goodfellow, Robin Hood, Hobgoblin. The charm given above proves that he was classed with wicked wights and evil spirits, and he is even alluded to as 'Some Robin the divell, or I wot not what spirit of the Ayre'.[3]

The opinion now generally accepted is that the present idea of fairies is due to Shakespeare. Up to this time English fairies were of the same type as in those countries where his influence has been less felt. In northern Scotland, in Ireland, and in France, especially in Brittany, the fairy is of the size of an ordinary human being and has all the characteristics of a human person. Shakespeare himself, in the *Merry Wives of Windsor*, makes Anne Page not only dress herself as a fairy but expect to be taken for one, though she was a full-grown young woman. There is plenty of literary evidence in the seventeenth century to show that a fairy could be mistaken for an ordinary mortal; and it was not until after the appearance of *A Midsummer Night's Dream* that the fairy began, in literature, to decrease to its present diminutive proportions. Literature, especially through the theatre, altered the popular conception of the old tradition, and the tiny elf of fancy drove out its human progenitor.

Descriptions of fairies given by eye-witnesses can be found in many accounts in the Middle Ages and slightly later. The sixteenth century was very prolific in such accounts. John Walsh,[4] the witch of Netherberry in Dorset, consulted the fairies between the hours of twelve and one at noon and at midnight, and always went among 'hills' for the purpose. Bessie Dunlop[5] in Ayrshire saw eight women and four men, 'the men were clad in gentlemen's clothing, and the women had all plaids round them and were very seemly-like to see'; she was informed that these were 'from the Court of Elfame'; she had previously received a visit from the Queen of Elfhame though without knowing at the time who her visitor was; she described the Queen as 'a stout woman who came in to her and sat down on the form beside her and asked a drink at her and she gave it.' Alesoun Peirsoun,[6] in Fifeshire, was 'convict for haunting and repairing with the good neighbours and Queen of Elphane, and she had many good friends at that court which were of her own blood, who had good acquaintance with the Queen of Elphane.' In Leith, Christian Livingstone[7] affirmed 'that her daughter was taken away with the fairy-folk, and that all the [occult] knowledge she had was by her daughter who met with the fairy.' Aberdeen was full of people who were well acquainted with fairies. One woman[8] told the judges that 'what skill so ever she has she had it of her mother, and her mother learned it at an elf-man.' Andro Man appears to have been the husband of the 'Queen of Elphen', with whom he had lived for thirty-two years and by whom he had several children. The seventeenth century was equally prolific in friends of the fairy. Jonet Drever[9] in Orkney was 'convict and guilty of the fostering of a bairn in the hill of Westray to the fairyfolk, called of her our good neighbours. And having conversation with the fairy twenty-six years bygone, in respect of her own confession.' The accused escaped with her life, but her sentence was, 'To be scourged from the end of the said town to the other. And thereafter to be banished the country. And never to return under pain of death.' Jean Weir,[10] sister of the celebrated witch, Major Weir, stated that 'when she kept a school at Dalkeith and teached children, a tall woman came to the declarant's house when the children were there; and that she had, as appeared to her, a child upon her back, and one or two at her foot; and that the said woman desired that the declarant should employ her to speak for her to the Queen of the Fairy, and strike and battle in her behalf with the said Queen (which was her own words).' The records of the Edinburgh Justiciary Court[11] gives an account of this transaction in a shorter and more sinister manner: 'Jean Weir took employment from a Woman to speak in her behalf to the Queen of ffarie, meaning the Devil.' In almost every case of so-called witchcraft, from Joan of Arc in 1431 down to the middle or end of the seventeenth century, the most damning evidence against the accused was acquaintance with the fairies; proof of such acquaintance meant, with very rare exceptions, condemnation to the stake. These fairies were not the little gossamer-winged flower-elves of children's tales, but creatures of flesh and blood, who inspired the utmost fear and horror among the comfortable burgher folk of the towns, and filled the priests and ministers of the Christian Church with the desire to exterminate them.

The number of recorded marriages between 'mortals' and fairies is another proof that fairies were the same size as ordinary folk and that they were human. The Plantagenet kings had a fairy ancestry; Conn, King of Tara, married a fairy as his second wife; Bertrand du Guesclin had a fairy wife, so also had that Sieur de Bourlemont who owned the Fairy Tree round which Joan of Arc danced as a girl. When a 'mortal' man married a fairy woman the children appear to have belonged to the father and to have been in no way different from the children of two 'mortals'. This was the case even when the fairy girl was carried off by force. Marriages between 'mortal' women and fairy men were also not infrequent; but unless the girl was captured and kept as a prisoner in the home of the fairies, she remained comfortably in her own village, where she was visited by her fairy husband, and the children were not to be distinguished from 'mortal' children. This shows that the cross between mortals and fairies was less distinguishable than one between members of a white and of a coloured race.

The accounts of fairies, when given by people who for various reasons were unaffected by the influence of Shakespeare, show them as real human beings, smaller than those who made the records but not very noticeably so. They lived in the wild uncultivated parts of the country, not necessarily because they were dispossessed by immigrants but more probably because they were originally entirely pastoral and unacquainted with agriculture. Though they might sometimes be found in woods they preferred open moors and heaths which afforded pasturage for their cattle. Like some of the wild tribes in India they fled from a stranger, were fleet of foot, and so highly skilled in the art of taking cover that they were seldom seen unless they so desired. Their dwelling-places were built of stone, wattle or turf, and were in bee-hive form, and here whole families lived together as in an Eskimo igloo. It is not impossible that the houses were in use in the winter only, and the fairy people lived entirely out of doors in the summer. For similar conditions of life the people of the Asiatic steppes afford the best parallel.

Like the people of the steppe the fairies appear to have lived chiefly on the milk of their herds, with an occasional orgy of a meat feast. In this they differed completely from the agriculturists who inhabited the more fertile parts of the country. The immense difference in physique caused by the introduction of grain into the regular diet of mankind is hardly yet realized except by the few who have studied the subject. It is not improbable that the small stature of the fairy, the stunted size of the changelings, the starved condition of the 'mortal' captive among the fairies, may have been due to the diet.

The accounts of the fairies, as preserved in legal records and in folklore, show a people whose parallel can be found, in western Europe, in the Neolithic and Bronze Ages. The skeletal remains in Neolithic burial-barrows prove that the people who then inhabited Great Britain were short in stature, the height of the men being about 5 feet 5 inches and the women proportionately less. They were long-headed and probably had dark complexions (hence perhaps the affectionate nickname of Brownie given to a kindly fairy).

In Great Britain the Neolithic and Bronze Age people lived on open downs and moors; they were chiefly pastoral, practising agriculture but rarely. They no longer lived in caves like Palaeolithic Man, but built houses or huts. These houses were circular in plan, and were sunk in the earth to the depth of two or three feet; the floor was paved with stone, and the lower part of the walls was of stone also; the upper part of the walls was of wattle-and-daub or of turf, and the roof was of turf supported by a central post which perhaps carried a wooden frame. The hearth, when there was one, was in the middle of the one chamber, and there was an opening in the roof to allow the smoke to escape. Such houses were built in groups; and when overgrown with grass, bracken and small shrubs would appear like mounds or small hills. The remains of Bronze Age houses, known as 'hut-circles', are not found in valleys or those parts which were covered with forest, they are in open grassy country. In those parts are found also the little flint arrow-heads which are commonly called 'elf-bolts', and are known to be of the Bronze Age.

A hut of the kind described above is shown on Plate 9, where it is called a 'fairy house', and as the two principal inhabitants wear crowns it must be the palace of the fairy king and queen. The hut is circular, is partly sunk below the surface of the ground and is roofed with turf on which shrubs are growing. It is one of a group of similar huts, which from the outside have the appearance of little hills or mounds, which is perhaps what John Walsh[4] meant when he said that he consulted the fairies on hills. The inhabitants are smaller than the man who is speaking to them, but they are not dwarfs or midgets. This then is clear evidence of the belief in elves and fairies at the date of the picture, i.e. 1555, and is proof not only of the human nature of the fairies and of their close resemblance to the Neolithic people but also of the survival of the Neolithic and Bronze Age folk and their civilization as late as the sixteenth century.

The fairies, then, were the descendants of the early people who inhabited northern Europe; they were pastoral but not nomad, they lived in the unforested parts of the country where there was good pasturage for their cattle, and they used stone in the Neolithic period and metal in the Bronze Age for their tools and weapons. Later on, when the fierce tribes of the Iron Age, the Kelts, poured into western Europe and to a great extent exterminated the people and the civilization of the Bronze Age, those folk who lived in the wild parts escaped the general massacre and learned that their best defence was to strike terror into the hearts of their savage neighbours. To them the new metal was part of the equipment of their formidable enemies and they held it in horror, but they still worked so well in bronze that their swords were coveted by the invaders. It was from our ancestors of the Iron Age that the traditional fear of the fairies was derived, the terror of the cunning and implacable enemy which is found in all records of fairies until Shakespeare dispersed it. Undoubtedly as civilization advanced and more land came under cultivation the fairy people must have mingled more and more with the settled population, till many of them entered the villages and became indistinguishable from the 'mortals'. It is the same process of absorption which is going on at the present day among the gypsies in Europe and the Bedawin of the Near East.

That the fairies, i.e. the witches, had settled in the villages is shown by the statements of the contemporary recorders. Sprenger[12] in the *Malleus Maleficarum* says that 'there is not so little a parish but there are many witches known to be therein.' In 1589 Remigius[13] states that to the best of his recollection there were not less than eight hundred witches condemned during the sixteen years that he was criminal judge in Lorraine; and that at least the same number either fled or prolonged their lives by enduring torture and torment without confession. De Lancre[14] says that 'the abomination' was spread throughout Europe so that France, England, Italy, Germany, and Spain were filled and overflowing with it. Bodin[15] notes that 'Satan has witches of every quality. He has kings, princes, priests, preachers, in many places the judges, doctors, in short he has them of all professions.' Still later Bishop Hall[16] remarks on a village in Lancashire where the number of witches was greater than the number of houses. This is proof that the religion was not originally confined only to the poor and ignorant but counted the highest ranks among its members. The fact that it was hereditary shows that it was universal; Bodin[17] is very emphatic on this point of an inherited cult, and urges all judges to use this knowledge as a method of catching unsuspected witches, and recommends that young girls should be seized and persuaded or frightened into compromising their relatives and friends. The only explanation of the immense numbers of witches who were legally tried and put to death in western Europe is that we are dealing with a religion which was spread over the whole continent and counted its members in every rank of society, from the highest to the lowest.

The complete absorption of the primitive population must have come to pass in England after the Black Death, when labour became so scarce that serfage was no longer possible and the feudal system broke down. The landlords, having land and no labour, let their farms to tenant-farmers, and these, owing to the high price of labour, took to sheep-farming. As the trade in wool prospered the number of flocks increased in proportion to the demand, to the great enrichment of the owners, till to the scandal of the old aristocracy the *nouveaux riches* of the Tudor period were raised to the peerage. Sheep require fewer men than cattle or field-work, and labourers were thrown out of work in such numbers that unemployment became a menace and a danger, and finally resulted in the Peasant Revolt. Sir Thomas More was the first to connect the unemployment of his day with the advent of a new type of industry, and he puts the matter very pithily when he says: 'The sheep have eaten up the men.' In grazing, the difference between cattle and sheep is very marked. For cattle the grass must be sufficiently long for the animal to put its tongue round a bunch of grass and break it off; the grass which is left is not bitten down to the roots. By the arrangement of their teeth sheep are able to nibble the grass almost to the roots; thus, sheep can graze after cattle but not cattle after sheep. Sheep can also find a living on ground which will not support cattle. As the fairies were cattle keepers the advent of the sheep must have driven them out of their old haunts; there would be no feed for their beasts as in the old days. To paraphrase Sir Thomas More, 'The sheep ate up the fairies.' More's remark was written in 1515; by the time Shakespeare began to write two generations at least had passed; the fairies were no more than a memory, believed in partly as human beings, partly as Little People on whom were fathered all the folk tales—horrible, pretty or comic—which were current. From this medley Shakespeare drew his inspiration with far-reaching results.

The theory that the fairies began as the Neolithic folk is supported by the Irish tradition of the Tuatha-da-Danann, who are the same as the English and Continental fairy-folk. They were 'great necromancers, skilled in all magic, and excellent in all arts as builders, poets and musicians.'[18] They were also great horse-breeders, stabling their horses in caves in the hills. When the Milesians, who seem to have been the people of the Bronze Age, invaded Ireland they endeavoured to exterminate the Tuatha, but by degrees the two races learned to live peaceably side by side.

With this theory in view it is worth while to examine the story of fairies in detail; it is then surprising to find how much has been recorded by eye-witnesses as to the appearance, dress and habits of the Little People. The houses are seldom described, for not only were they difficult to find, being carefully concealed, but the owners did not welcome visitors of another race. A parallel people are the Kurumbas of the Neilgherry Hills in South India. They are small in stature, their leaf-built houses are almost invisible in the jungles in which they are hidden, and the people themselves are said to be possessed of terrible magical powers, for which they are greatly feared by the neighbouring races. Much of what is written of the Kurumbas by modern investigators might be a description of the fairies, even more so are the stories of them in the traditions of their more civilized neighbours.

The fairies had a disconcerting habit of appearing and disappearing when least expected, a habit which seemed magical to the slow-moving heavy-footed agriculturists of the villages. Yet dexterity in taking cover was only natural in a people who must often have owed their lives to quickness of movement and ability to remain motionless. In Scott's 'Lady of the Lake' there is a description of Highlanders rising from ambush in an apparently uninhabited glen:

> *From shingles gray their lances start,*
> *The bracken bush sends forth the dart,*
> *The rushes and the willow wand*
> *Are bristling into axe and brand,*
> *And every tuft of broom gives life*
> *To plaided warrior armed for strife.*

Kipling in his 'Ballad of East and West' describes a similar faculty of complete invisibility among the Indian borderers:

> *There is rock to the left and rock to the right, and low lean thorn between,*
> *And ye may hear a breech-bolt snick where never a man is seen.*

These primitive people or fairies were spread across the country in little communities, each governed by its own ruler, as in modern Africa. Lady Wilde notes that every district in Ireland had its peculiar and separate fairy chief or king.[19] Occasionally the names of the fairy kings and queens have survived.[20]

From the great importance of the queen in the community it would seem that she was the real ruler and that the king had only a secondary place, except perhaps in case of war. Property appears to have been communal, consequently marriage laws were non-existent, as was the case among the Picts; and the fairy-queen in particular was never bound to one husband only. This laxness of morals may have been one reason why the Christian Church, which laboured so hard to introduce some kind of regularity into the marital relations among all the nations over which it had influence, so hated the fairies. *'Vrais diables incorporez'* Boguet calls them with a fierceness quite incomprehensible if the fairies were really only the imaginary tiny beings of our nursery tales. If, however, they were a Pagan population whose religion and customs were definitely contrary to the teaching of the Christian priests, the indignation of the Church would naturally be directed against them and their influence. To have communication with these 'incarnate devils' was to proclaim oneself an enemy of Christianity, and the offender would be treated with the utmost rigour by all Christian priests.

The conditions of life in the Neolithic and Bronze Age settlements are fairly well known; the people practised a little agriculture but in some parts were entirely pastoral. They owned all the domestic animals, but cattle were their mainstay. Isobel Gowdie[21] in 1662 claimed to have gone into a fairy hill 'and got meat there from the Queen of Fairy. There was elf-bulls routing and skoyling up and down there and affrighted me.' These bulls made a great impression on her mind for in a further confession she said, 'We went in to the Downie hills; the hill opened, and we came to a fair and large braw room in the day time. There are elf-bulls routing and skoyling there at the entry, which feared me.' Dogs of the Chow type were kept by the Neolithic people as watch-dogs; skeletons of such dogs have been found on Neolithic sites. Dogs are also mentioned in the tales of the fairies, fierce dogs who guarded the fairy hill. The paucity of agriculture among the fairy people is shown partly by the fact that cultivated land is not mentioned in connection with them, they are associated only with meadows; and partly by the fact that their powers were manifested on cattle, very rarely on crops. This evidence is corroborated by the situation of the known settlements of these periods; they are on open downs and moors, totally unsuited for the primitive plough then in use, though admirably adapted for grazing.

The Worshippers

There is still a considerable body of evidence as to the appearance and dresses of the fairies. Their garments appear to have varied not only according to the tribe to which the wearers belonged, but also to the rank which they held in their community. Eye-witnesses aver that the fairies spun and wove their own cloth. The fairy women were very notable spinners and could more than hold their own against a 'mortal', but their looms were not so satisfactory, and there are many stories extant of the fairies entering a cottage and weaving their cloth on the cottager's loom. The yarn used was generally wool and was occasionally undyed (called *loughtyn* in the Isle of Man), more often it was green or blue. The colours were dark as in the hunting-tartans of the Highlands, and the extremely dark blue gave rise to the belief in the black fairies. As John Walsh[22] (1566) expresses it, 'There be three kindes of fairies, the black, the white, and the green, of which the black be the woorst.' A century later Isobel Gowdie[23] volunteered the information that 'the queen of Fairy is brawly clothed in white linens, and in white and brown clothes, etc., and the king of Fairy is a braw man, well favoured, and broad-faced, etc.' It is most unfortunate that the recording clerk always put 'etc.' when Isobel began to give any real details about the fairies. Possibly he was afraid to record any information about those terrifying people.

The colours of the fairies' dresses were due to dyes, produced and used like those still employed in country places. The number of indigenous plants from which dye-stuffs are obtained is surprisingly large, such plants are to be found in all parts of the British Isles and the dyes cover the whole range of colour. Lichens give very fine dyes, red, yellow and blue; besides these, other plants and trees have been in use from time immemorial and dyes are still made from their roots, bark, leaves and fruit. All combinations of colour and shade can be made by mixing the dyes, but it is perhaps worth noting that there is no record of yellow being worn by the fairies; blue, black, green, and a little red, were the chief colours. Green was the favourite colour, the reason, probably being that the fairies were originally hunters, and green made them less visible to their quarry. Later, when they themselves were hunted, green was the best colour in which to move unobserved in a forest or to lie hidden on a moor. White garments are often recorded; these were probably of linen bleached in the sun. In many stories there are accounts of the fairies spreading their linen on the grass, and the extraordinary whiteness of the material is always the subject of admiration. Isobel Gowdie in the passage quoted above, appears to have been struck with the Fairy Queen's white garments.

The fairy men of lower rank wore trousers and jackets, the women skirts and bodices. The most characteristic article of attire, however, for all ranks was the hat, cap, or hood. This was so precious to a fairy that any of them would risk capture or pay any ransom to recover it if it fell into alien hands. The cap varied in shape and colour according to the district. In the West Highlands[24] the green conical caps of the fairies were like the rush helmets which children made, and like those commonly worn by Swedish Lapps. In Ireland[25] a fairy-man was 'like a boy of ten or twelve years old, only more broad and bulky, dressed in a grey little coat, and stockings of the same colour, with an old little black woollen hat.' In the Isle of Man[26] the fairies were dressed in undyed wool with little pointed red caps. In Wales[27] the male fairies had 'red-tripled caps and the ladies a light fantastic head-dress which waved in the wind.' The fairies of Upper Brittany[28] wore a kind of cap 'like a crown, which seemed to be part of their person.' At Hildesheim[29] the local goblin was dressed like a peasant, but so invariably wore a hood that he was called Hedekin or Hutkin. Even so far away as eastern Europe a Slav story[30] gives an account of a man who saw 'two little demons pulling each other's hair. By the cut of their short waistcoats, by their tight pantaloons and their three-cornered hats, he knew that they were inhabitants of the nether world.'

Fairies of higher rank were naturally better dressed. The

king and queen, when riding in procession, wore rich garments and were always crowned; on less solemn occasions
they were dressed like their subjects though in richer
materials. When, in a domestic emergency in the Royal
Household, the Fairy Queen went herself to borrow a basin-
ful of oatmeal from a cottage woman, she was dressed in the
richest green embroidered with gold and wore a small coronet
of pearls. Her servant, who returned the oatmeal, is simply
recorded as being in green. This was in Kirkcudbright-
shire.[31]

Fairy ladies of rank wore long flowing dresses which fell
to the ground in soft, sweeping folds; these robes were usually white, sometimes green, and occasionally scarlet. The
hair was loose over the shoulders, which increased the beauty
of the younger ladies, but the long straggling elf-locks of the
older women are always commented on with horror by the
'mortal' beholder. The fairy ladies covered their hair with
a veil or hood, and often wore a small coronet of gold. The
fairy knights wore gold or silver armour in battle or in
solemn processions; for ordinary wear they dressed in green
with a hat or cap; and on all occasions they wore green
cloaks or mantles, possibly arranged like a plaid.

When going among the villagers the records show that
the fairies were dressed like their neighbours, apparently lest
they should attract attention and so be recognized. Bessie
Dunlop[32] (1576) did not know till long afterwards that the
'stout woman' who visited her was actually the Queen of
Elfhame. There are also innumerable stories of 'mortals'
entering a fairy knowe and thereby becoming acquainted
with the appearance of some of the fairies whom they recognized later among the villagers; such recognition invariably
met with severe punishment. The fairy-woman of modern
Ireland is described as being like a respectable house-keeper
dressed in black; and as it is impossible to distinguish these
terrible and terrifying visitants from ordinary folk by their
appearance and dress, it is advisable not to admit a stranger
to the house or to show hospitality to an unknown visitor

while any serious domestic work, such as churning, is in progress, lest the stranger should prove to be one of the Good People.

A little is known of the tools and domestic implements of the fairy folk. They possessed spindles, but a spinning-wheel is never mentioned; weaving was practised, but there is no record of looms. Pottery, not metal, must have been generally used for domestic purposes as there are numerous stories of the fairies borrowing metal vessels which were punctually returned, often with a gift as repayment for the loan. In passing it may be noted that the fairies were scrupulous in keeping a promise, in which they were better than the 'mortals' who often cheated them. They were also grateful for kindnesses and repaid a debt of money or help generously. In Northumberland the fairies were definitely mortal, for they died and lie buried in Brinkburn under a green mound.[33]

The characteristic weapon of the fairies, and one which still bears their name, is the stone arrow-head or elf-bolt. These arrow-heads are made of flint and are found on open heaths and downs where the fairy people dwelt. They are now known to be of the Bronze Age. They are so small and slight that they could have been used only with a small and light bow, such as that carried by the masked dancer of the palaeolithic times (Plate 3). A little light weapon of this kind could have been of little value against a human enemy or a wild beast, the arrow could inflict hardly more than a flesh wound. The recorded method of using the arrow-heads, and one quite as ineffective as the little bow, was to spang them with the thumb as boys shoot a marble. Yet to be shot with an elf-bolt meant death or at least severe illness, usually paralysis. The only theory which explains the terror in which this puny weapon was held is that it was poisoned. A slight wound inflicted by the sharp point would be sufficient to introduce the poison into the system; and in the case of human beings, fright would do the rest. Domestic animals seldom died of elf-shot if remedies were applied within a reasonable time, the result being then only a few days' illness;

but if neglected the creature died. Poisoned arrows[34] are actually recorded, 'The fairy arrows were made of bog-reed, tipped with white flints, and dipped in the dew of hemlock.' It is not unlikely that the use of poisoned darts was a legacy from Palaeolithic times; it was probably one of the means by which primitive man was able to destroy his fourfooted enemies. The common poisonous plants of the fields and woods are often deadly when distilled and then introduced into the system through a wound. A couple of hunters with a good stock of poisoned arrows could have kept a pack of wolves at bay, for the poison acts with great rapidity. There is still extant the evidence of an eye-witness that fairy arrows were being made, and used by their makers, in the seventeenth century. In 1662 Isobel Gowdie[35] records, 'As for Elf arrow-heads, the Devil shapes them with his own hands, and then delivers them to elf-boys, who whet and dight them with a sharp thing like a packing-needle.' Isobel found that it required practice to spang an arrow with her thumb, for though she claimed to have hit and killed a ploughman she missed the Laird of Park when she shot at him. The poisoned arrows could not have been used for killing game or food animals as the poison remains in the body and is not removed by cooking. Game was probably run down by the hunters on foot, as is still done by the Bedawin of the Near East.

The Little People are not recorded as having used any other weapon than the arrow against human beings; they seem to have fought with spears among themselves, and they made bronze swords of extraordinary efficacy. In the story of Gisli, the sword Graysteel was forged by the dwarfs (i.e. the fairies), and it could therefore cut through whatever its blow fell on, nor could its edge be blunted by spells like swords made by mortals. A fairy javelin[36] was preserved at Midridge Hall in the county of Durham, but there is unfortunately no legend to account for its coming into the possession of a mortal.

A certain amount of tangible evidence as to the existence of fairies still remains in the form of objects of fairy work-

manship, which have come in various ways into the possession of 'mortals'. Gervase of Tilbury and William of New-
bury record how a cup was once stolen by a man from a
fairy; it was 'of an unknown material, extraordinary colour,
and unusual form'. It was given by the stealer to the Earl of
Gloucester, and by him presented to Henry I, who in his
turn gave it to his Queen's brother, David of Scotland; after
remaining many years in the Scotch treasury it was presented
by William the Lion to Henry II. In Kirk Malew, in the
Isle of Man,[37] the silver chalice was a cup stolen from the
fairies; a similar story is told of other places. The Luck of
Edenhall is a painted glass cup; it came into the possession
of the family through the butler, who accidentally surprised
a party of fairies at a feast; the terrified fairies fled leaving
the cup behind. At Frensham, in Surrey, there is a huge
metal cauldron which is said to have been borrowed from the
fairies and never returned. In Scotland the banner of the
Macdonalds is well known, it was presented to the head of
the clan by the fairies. Though no proof can be adduced that
these objects were made by fairy hands the tradition that
they were so made shows the belief that, in later times at any
rate, the fairies were as skilful in working metal and stone
and in weaving textiles as any human being, and that the
objects which they made are as solid and tangible as any
others of that period.

If then my theory is correct we have in the medieval
accounts of the fairies a living tradition of the Neolithic and
Bronze Age people who inhabited western Europe. With
further study it might be possible to show the development
of their civilization, first by the contact between the flint-
users and the bronze-workers, then by the slow development
of intercourse with the people of the Iron Age, by whose
descendants they were finally absorbed. The last authentic
account of the fairies occurs in Scotland at the end of the
seventeenth century, but in England they had disappeared
long before. This strange and interesting people and their
primitive civilization have degenerated into the diminutive

gossamer-winged sprites of legend and fancy, and occur only in stories to amuse children. The real upland-dweller, who struck terror into the lowlanders and horrified the priests of the Christian faith, has vanished utterly.

6a. CERNUNNOS

On a Roman Altar, Cluny Museum, Paris

6b. THE WITCHES' KITCHEN

Belgian medieval fire-back

(By kind permission of the Director of Virton Museum)

7. WORSHIP OF THE HORNED GOD IN
ANCIENT EGYPT

The Priesthood

*'A witch is a person that hath conference with the Devil to take
counsel or to do some act.'*—LORD COKE

In all organized religions, even those of the Lower
Culture, there is a priesthood, and the more organized
the religion the more systematized does the priesthood
become. Early priesthoods appear to have been largely composed of women; as the religion changed, men gradually took
over the practice of the ritual. This is clear in Egypt, where
the early inscriptions mention many priesthoods of women;
in the later inscriptions women are only singers in the
temple. But when a religion is decaying and a new one taking
its place the women often remain faithful and carry on the
old rites, being then obliged to act as priestesses.

These changes are seen in the cult of the Horned God.
In the Palaeolithic paintings there is only one scene which
can be identified as a religious ceremony performed by
several persons. This is at Cogul, in north-eastern Spain, and
represents a dance of nine women round a standing male
figure (Plate 10). A similar dance, also round a standing male
figure dates from the seventeenth century, but in this there
are as many men as women (Plate 11).

Cotton Mather, in his account of the Salem witches in
1692,[1] states that 'the witches do say that they form themselves much after the manner of Congregational Churches,
and that they have a Baptism, and a Supper, and Officers
among them, abominably resembling those of our Lord.'
His statement is abundantly proved by the evidence in the
trials, and the priesthood can be recognized in the *covens*.
The word coven was used both in England and Scotland to

designate a band of people of both sexes, who were always in close attendance on their god, who went to all the meetings, large or small, who performed the ceremonies either alone or in company with the Grandmaster, and who were conspicuous in the ritual. To them the god taught the prayers they were to say, to them he gave his counsel and help in a special manner, and in all the rites and ceremonies they were near his person. In short, they were set apart to perform the duties and ceremonies always associated with priests and priestesses, and must be regarded as the priesthood of the Horned God. It is probably this body to which Reginald Scot[2] refers when he mentions that the witch went through three admission ceremonies. The first was when she accepted the Devil's invitation to join the society, 'they consent privily, and come not into the fairies' assembly'(the connection of witches and fairies should be noted). 'The order of their bargain or profession is double; the one solemn and public, the other secret and private.' This seems to indicate that after the public profession of faith, such as all converts had to make, the priestess was admitted by a special and private rite. De Lancre makes the statement that 'there are two sorts of witches, the first sort are composed of witches who, having abandoned God, give themselves to drugs and poisons. The second are those who have made an expresss renunciation of Jesus Christ and of the Faith and have given themselves to Satan. These perform wonders'[3].

It was this body of persons who were specially stigmatized as witches in the sixteenth and seventeenth centuries, and to describe them the Christian recorders ransacked their vocabularies for invectives and abusive epithets. The favourite adjectives to apply to witches and their doings were: hellish, diabolical, devilish, infernal, abominable, horrible. A fine blood-curdling effect can be built up by a judicious use of such epithets, especially when accompanied by capital letters. Thus Black Magic has a more sinister appearance than the same words written in ordinary characters; a Hellish Altar raised on Infernal Columns or a Rampant Hag attending a

Diabolical Sacrament sound more wicked than if the description were couched in more moderate language. In the same way the Chief or Grandmaster was more horror-striking and awful when called Satan, the Foul Fiend, the Enemy of Salvation, the Prince of Darkness, or other epithet of the kind than when soberly alluded to as the Man in Black. The effect could be heightened by using black-letter type for these names, as Glanvil does. When the right atmosphere of horror was attained by these means, the reader's mind was prepared to accept as evidence much that would have been rejected if set before him in a coldly critical manner. This atmosphere, however, remains in the minds of many people at the present day, the old abusive style holds good yet, the acts of the witches are still attributed to 'occult' powers, to their conference with the Foul Fiend, the Principle of Evil; and to dissipate the fog which the words of the Christian recorders have created is still a task of some difficulty.

There were large numbers of adherents of the Old Faith who were never brought before the Inquisitors, for it seems that to a great extent the persecution was against the members of the covens, who were regarded as devil-worshippers and enemies of Christ, and were accused of practising hellish rites and of having dealings with infernal powers. No matter whether the magic was used for good only, if an accused person belonged to a coven the doom was certain. This explanation accounts for the numerous cases of men and women of good and kindly lives, whose so-called witchcraft was practised for the benefit of others, yet they were remorselessly hunted down and put to death. Joan of Arc at one end of the series and the Salem witches at the other died for their Faith, not for their acts. Bodin[4] goes so far as to say, 'Even if the witch has never killed or done evil to man, or beast, or fruits, and even if he has always cured bewitched people, or driven away tempests, it is because he has renounced God and treated with Satan that he deserves to be burned alive.' And he goes on,[5] 'Even if there is no more than the obligation to the Devil, having denied God, this deserves the most cruel death that can be imagined.'

The number in a coven never varied, there were always thirteen, i.e. twelve members and the god. In the small districts there would be only one coven; where the means of communication were easy and the population large there would be a coven in each village, but instead of the god himself there would be a man or woman who acted for the Grandmaster and conducted the services in his name. When all the covens met at the Great Sabbaths and the Grandmaster was present in person, the substitutes were called 'officers'. There is some evidence to show that on the death of a Grandmaster his place was filled either by election or by seniority from among the officers. In the witch-trials the existence of covens appears to have been well known, for it is often observable how the justices and the priests or ministers of religion pressed the unfortunate prisoners to inculpate their associates, but after persons to the number of thirteen or any multiple of thirteen had been brought to trial, or had at least been accused, no further trouble was taken in the matter. There is a statement on this custom by one of the leading legal authorities[6] who wrote in the middle of the seventeenth century; he says that the Devil treated certain members of his congregation differently from others, 'the Precepts of Witchcraft are not delivered indifferently to every Man, but to his own subjects, and not to them all but to special and tried ones.' This is also probably the reason why Lord Coke defined a witch as 'a person who hath conference with the Devil to take counsel or to do some act.'

The number thirteen seems to have had some special meaning in pre-Christian times. To mention only two out of a great number; Romulus, who was both king and Incarnate God, went about surrounded by his twelve lictors; and the Danish hero, Hrolf, was always accompanied by his twelve berserks. Both are legendary personages; Hrolf was within the Christian era though himself a Pagan, but Romulus was most certainly pre-Christian, and his legend could not therefore be contaminated by Christian beliefs. There is reason then to consider that the covens of the Horned God took their rise before the introduction of Christianity into the world.

There is only one trial in which the number thirteen is specifically mentioned, when Isobel Gowdie[7] stated that in each coven of her district there were thirteen persons. In the other trials the number is indicated and can be recovered by counting up the accused persons. As I have noted above, the Old Religion held its place longer among the women than among the men. The coven of Romulus consisted of thirteen men; if the legendary companions of Robin Hood[8] were real personages, then that coven was composed of twelve men and one woman; Gilles de Rais (1440)[9] had eleven men and two women, Bessie Dunlop (1567)[10] spoke of five men and eight women, and in Kinross-shire (1662)[11] one man and twelve women formed the coven.

The Incarnate God, called the Devil by the Christian recorders, was the supreme chief of the coven; the second in command was known as the Officer, who represented the Chief in his absence, and there was besides a woman-member called the 'Maiden'.[12] All offices could be held by women, including that of Chief, though they were usually filled by men, except of course that of the Maiden, who was always a woman. In England women appear to have some-times doubled the offices of deputy-chief and of Maiden. Wherever she is recorded the Maiden appears as a more important person than the Officer and as ranking next to the Grandmaster though without executive power. She sat at the right hand of the Incarnate God at feasts, and she generally led the dance with him. If, as I maintain, Joan of Arc belonged to the Old Religion her title of La Pucelle, the Maid, takes a new significance and emphasizes her position in regard to her royal master, for she was not only Maid of Orleans but bore the higher title of La Pucelle de France.

To any member of the coven might be deputed the task of summoner. In a small district the Chief himself would notify all members as to the place where the *Esbat* or weekly meeting would be held; but in a large district a member, well known to the whole coven, went from house to house with the information. 'Many times himself warneth them to meet, sometimes he appointeth others to warn them in his stead',[13] as was the case with Robert Grieve of Lauder in 1649, 'the Devil gave him that charge, to be his officer to warn all to the meetings.'[14] The summoner, whether Chief or ordinary member, was careful to be inconspicuous when employed in this way. In Renfrewshire this secrecy was carried further than usual, 'for particular warning there appeared a Black Dog with a Chain about his Neck, who tinkling it, they were to follow.'[15]

The duties of the officer were varied; he was often the summoner, he arranged for the meetings and saw that due notice was given, he kept the records of attendance and of work done, he presented new members and informed the Chief of any likely convert. If the Chief did not choose to dance the officer led the ring; and if the officer were also a Christian priest, as was not uncommon, he performed part of the religious service.

The musician was another important member of coven. The Chief was often the performer, sitting in the centre of the ring and playing on the pipes, the flute or the Jews' harp. Jonet Lucas of Aberdeen[16] in 1597 was accused that 'thou and they was under the conduct of thy master the Devil, dancing in a ring, and he playing melodiously upon an instrument.' On another occasion Isobel Cockie of the same coven did not approve of the Devil's playing, 'thou wast the ringleader, next Thomas Leyis, and because the Devil played not so melodiously and well as thou crewit, thou took the instrument out of his mouth, then took him on the chaps therewith and played thyself thereon to the whole company.' As a rule, however, the musician did not dance the round dance but sat outside the ring (Plate 11), though in the long dance he was often the leader.

The organization was very complete, each coven being independent under its own officer, yet linked with all the other covens of the district under one Grandmaster. This was the system, which in all probability was followed by Augustine when he 'placed bishops in every place where there had been flamens, and archbishops where there had been arch-flamens.'

A coven could act alone or, when numbers were needed, could combine with others. For a combined effort the witches of North Berwick afford one of the best examples.[17] There were thirty-nine men and women, i.e. three covens, who met together to aid their Master in destroying James VI of Scotland. Some raised the storm, some undertook the slow destruction of the wax image, some prepared the toad poison, and some arranged to get a garment which the king had worn. These duties were more than the members of one coven could manage, and they were obliged to have help from the other covens under the domination of the one Master.

Recruiting for the religion was not required while the cult was in its prime, but as the Church gained power and began to persecute there was difficulty in obtaining converts, and judging by the statements of the witches a Chief had often to use persuasion and bribery to secure a likely recruit. Once secured it was difficult for the member to withdraw, for discipline was strict within the coven. In most places the Master ruled through the love which the members bore to himself as the Incarnate God, for as de Lancre[18] puts it, 'the Devil so holds their hearts and wills that he hardly allows any other desire to enter therein.' This personal affection of the worshipper for the God must always be taken into account in considering the cult of the Horned God. 'The love of God' was no *façon de parler* among the witches but was a vital force in their lives.

This passionate clinging to their own religion and their own god was regarded by the Christian recorders as blasphemy and devilish obstinacy. Bodin says,[19] 'Satan promises that they shall be so happy after this life that it prevents their repenting and they die obstinate in their wickedness.' De

Lancre[20] wrote in the same strain when he urged the lay
judges to have no pity on the patience of witches under torture, 'it is the Devil alone who furnishes the means, this
patience is a forced obstinacy without merit, which can bring
no other reward than the eternal agony of hell-fire.' In
England the facts are often recorded in some detail. Rose
Hallybread and Rebecca West[21] 'died very stubborn and
refractory, without any remorse or seeming terror of conscience for their abominable witchcraft.' The witches of
Northamptonshire[22] were particularly loyal to their god.
Agnes Brown and her daughter, after they were condemned
to death, 'were carried back to gaol where they were never
heard to pray or to call upon God, but with bitter curses and
execrations spent the little time they had to live, until the
day of their execution, when never asking pardon for their
offences whether of God or the world, in this their dangerous
and desperate resolution, died.' Elinor Shaw and Mary
Phillips of the same coven at their execution 'being desired
to say their prayers, they both set up a very loud Laughter,
calling for the Devil to come and help them in such a Blasphemous manner, as is not fit to Mention; so that the Sherif
seeing their presumptuous Impenitence, caused them to be
Executed with all the Expedition possible; even while they
were Cursing and raving, and as they liv'd the Devil's true
Factors, so they resolutely Dyed in his Service.' The remaining members of the coven died 'without any confession or
contrition.' In Guernsey in 1563, Martin Tulouff[23] and
Colinette Gascoing refused the pardon of God and the queen.

There was in all places a system of rewards and punishments; these are noted only when the religion was falling
into decay. Praise awarded publicly before the assembled
coven, the honour of leading the dance with the Master, and
gifts of money were the usual rewards. Punishments consisted of public rebukes for minor offences; for more serious
faults beating was the most usual method of correction, this
might be inflicted by blows from the Chief's fist or from a
stick wielded by the Chief's hand. Many a transgressing

member of a coven must have returned home black and blue with bruises as a reminder that implicit obedience was the Chief's due.

It was not till the religion became a secret matter and the persecution of the Church was pressing it hard, that capital punishment first appeared. This was inflicted on actual or potential traitors, whose treachery might involve the safety of other members of the coven, more especially that of the Master. The almost invariable method of execution was by strangulation, and often occurred in the prison in which the suspected traitor was guarded. After death a thin string or other totally inadequate ligature was tied loosely round the neck in such a way as to show that the victims had not died by their own hand but had been done to death as an act of justice. Though the Christian recorders generally sum up the event with the words 'and thus the Devil killed him in prison', there is one record which shows clearly how the execution was effected. The man-witch Playfair[24] was consulted by the mother of Robert, Earl of Lothian, about a cancer in her breast. He cured her by casting the disease on her husband who died of cancer in the throat. In 1597 'the said Playfair, being soon apprehended, was made prisoner in Dalkeith steeple, and having confest that and much more wickedness to Mr. Archibald Simson, minister there, and that confession coming to the ears of Robert, Earl of Lothian, my lord's son, he had moyen to get some persons admitted to speak with the prisoner in the night, by which meanes he was found *worried* [strangled] in the morning, and the point of his breeches knit about his neck, but never more enquiry was made who had done the deed.'

The importance of the lace or string among the witches was very great as it was the insignia of rank. The usual place to carry it on the person was round the leg where it served as a garter. The beliefs of modern France give the clue as to its importance.[25] According to traditions still current, there is a fixed number of witches in each canton, of whom the chief wears the garter in token of his (or her) high position;

the right of becoming chief is said to go by seniority. In Haute Bretagne[26] a man who makes a pact with the Devil has a red garter. The red garter figures also in one of Croker's stories of Irish fairies,[27] 'The Cluricane showed Tom where the crock of gold was buried under a big *boliaun* (ragwort). Tom tied his red garter round it to recognize it again, while he went to fetch his spade. On his return he found every boliaun in the field had a red garter tied to it.' Here the garter had obviously been used as a means of magic by a man who had no right to do so and it was therefore entirely ineffectual.

These are the modern examples, but in the sixteenth and seventeenth centuries the garter played a more sinister part. I have already quoted the account of the death of the man Playfair, where cause and effect are clearly indicated, the punishment for treachery following hard on the betrayal. As it was a man of high rank who had instigated the murder 'never more enquiry was made who had done the deed.' At the same time it is possible that the Earl of Lothian may have been the chief of a coven and have been feared accordingly. Fear certainly prevented further enquiry in the case of the man-witch John Stewart in 1618.[28] He was in prison on the charge of being a witch, and was so fettered that in his own words he could not raise his hand 'to take off my bonnet nor to get bread to my mouth.' Half an hour before the trial began he was visited by two ministers of religion. They had hardly left when the officers of the court were sent to bring him before the justices; they found him already dead, strangled 'with a tait of hemp (or string made of hemp, supposed to have been his garter or string of his bonnet).' He was carried out into the air and all means were used to bring him round, 'but he revived not, but so ended his life miserable by the help of the devil his master.' In 1696 John Reid in Renfrewshire[29] was in prison awaiting his trial for witchcraft, he was asked one night 'whether he desired company or would be afraid alone, he said he had no fear of anything.' The next morning he was found strangled, with his own neckcloth tied loosely round his neck and fastened to a small stick stuck into a hole above the chimneypiece. 'It was concluded that some extraordinary Agent had done it, especially considering that the Door of the Room was secured, and that there was a board set over the Window which was not there the night before when they left him.' These executions give a special meaning to Gilles de Rais' outburst of contempt against the ecclesiastical court assembled to try him on a charge of witchcraft, that he 'would rather be hanged in a lace than submit to their jurisdiction.'[30]

A string—as a garter, a 'point', or in the cap—was an ordinary part of the dress, and it is very remarkable how often it is mentioned in the descriptions of the Devil's costume. The Scotch Thom Reid[31] wore a cap 'close behind and plain before, with silken laces through the lips thereof'; the Lancashire Mamilion[32] was in a suit of black tied about with silk points; the Swedish Antecessor[33] had red and blue stockings with long garters. The importance of the garter is shown in the witch dance of the Palaeolithic painting (Plate 10), where the male figure, who stands in the centre, wears a garter on each leg standing out on either side of the knees. It seems therefore not unlikely that the string was a symbol of authority worn on a part of the person where it would be visible to all and yet would not impede in any way the movements of the wearer.

The garter has long been credited with magical properties, especially when belonging to a woman. The bride's garters were fought for at a wedding, and the Mettye Belt was always a man-witch's belt or a woman-witch's garter. The Mettye Belt was the recognized magical means of ascertaining whether a sick person would recover or not; it was put round the patient's body and the augury obtained from it. It was of this magical practice that the unfortunate Janet Pereson[34] was accused in Durham in 1570; the charge against her stated that 'she uses witchcraft in measuring of belts to preserve folks from the fairy.' As late as the eighteenth century the magical power of the garter is well illustrated in a story from the Orkneys,[35] 'There was an eagle flew up with a cock at Scalloway, which one of these enchanters seeing, presently took a string (his garter as was supposed), and casting some knots thereupon with the using the ordinary words, the eagle did let fall the cock into the sea.'

The garter in legend can be of great importance. The story attached to the castle of Sewingshields, in Northumberland,[36] states that in a cave under the castle sleep King Arthur, Queen Guinevere, their courtiers, and thirty couple of hounds. A farmer found his way into the cave, and on a stone table near the entrance he saw a stone sword, a garter and a horn. He picked up the sword, cut the garter, then his heart failed as he saw the sleepers awaking. As he hurried out of the cave he heard King Arthur say, 'O woe befall the evil day that ever the witless wight was born, who took the sword, the garter cut, but never blew the bugle-horn.' Strutt states that in the ninth century cross-gartering seems to have been confined to 'kings and princes, or the clergy of the highest order, and to have formed part of their state habit.'[37] Later in the Middle Ages the garter had obviously a significance which it does not possess now. The *Liber Niger* records that Richard I animated his army at the siege of Acre by giving to certain chosen knights leather garters to tie about their legs.

The extraordinarily circumstantial tradition of the foundation of the Order of the Garter in the reign of Edward III also emphasizes its importance. The story—which every child has heard—relates that a lady, either the Fair Maid of Kent or the Countess of Salisbury, dropped her garter while dancing with Edward III, that she was overcome with confusion, that the king picked up the garter, fastened it on his own leg with the words *Honi soit qui mal y pense*, and at once founded the Order of the Garter with twenty-six knights in honour of the event, that Order being from the beginning the highest of all knightly Orders in Europe. Though the story may be apocryphal there is a substratum of truth in it. The confusion of the Countess was not from the shock to her modesty—it took more than a dropped garter to shock a lady of the fourteenth century—but the possession of that garter proved that she was not only a member of the Old Religion but that she held the highest place in it. She therefore stood in imminent danger from the Church which had already started on its career of persecution. The king's quickness and presence of mind in donning the garter might have saved the immediate situation, but the action does not explain his words nor the foundation of the commemorative Order. If, however, the garter was the insignia of the chieftainship of the Old Religion, he thereby placed himself in the position of the Incarnate God in the eyes of his Pagan subjects. And it is noteworthy that he swiftly followed up the action by the foundation of an order of twelve knights for the King and twelve for the Prince of Wales, twenty-six members in all, in other words two covens. Froissart's words seem to imply that Edward understood the underlying meaning of the Garter, 'The King told them it should prove an excellent expedient for the uniting not only of his subjects one with another, but all Foreigners conjunctively with them in the Bonds of Amity and Peace.' It is remarkable that the King's mantle as Chief of the Order was powdered over with one hundred and sixty-eight garters which, with his own Garter worn on the leg, makes 169, or thirteen times thirteen, i.e. thirteen covens.

The Meetings. There were two classes of meetings, the Esbats which were specially for the covens, and the Sabbaths which were for the congregation as a whole.

The Esbats took place weekly, though not always on the same day of the week nor in the same place. They were for both religious and business purposes. Attendance at the Esbat was compulsory for the coven, but other members of the congregation were admitted to the religious rites. Thus the French witches, Antoine Tornier and Jaquema Paget,[38] returning from gleaning one day, saw a meeting being held in a field called Longchamois; they laid down their bundles, joined in the meeting, and when it was over they picked up their bundles and went home. It is not uncommon at the present day to see women stop and join in a religious service on their way home from work, exactly as Antoine and Jaquema did, but as the modern woman attends a Christian service and the witches attended a Pagan rite the former are called devout and the latter are devil-worshippers.

The business part of the Esbats and Sabbaths consisted of reports from the members of their work during the previous week and of their proposed work in the days to follow. Isobel Gowdie (1662) stated that 'all our acts and deeds, betwixt great meetings, must be given account of and noted in his book at each Grand meeting.'[39] They consulted with the Chief or with his deputy as to any matters in which advice was needed. These matters were usually cases of illness, for the witches of a coven were always the healers in a village. There were also cases of divination in which direction was required, and by the reports of the witches the Chief was kept informed of all that went on in his district and was able to give help or reproof where needed. A newly-made member of the coven would receive instruction at the Esbat, either from the Chief or from a fellow-member, such instruction including methods of divination by animals. Sometimes the Chief himself desired help and he then chose his assistants from among those present. If a new remedy or charm were to be tried the whole coven was instructed and the result, successful or otherwise, had to be reported at the next meeting. Included in the business was information as to likely converts. The members themselves were always ready to put in a word to those who were discontented with Christianity, and the Master or one of the officers could then take the case in hand. After the business was finished the coven turned to its religious celebrations. Though the Chief sometimes gave an address, in which he laid down and explained the dogmas of the religion, the main ceremony was the sacred dance. After this came the feast, which was often followed by another dance, then the meeting broke up and the members returned home.

The Priesthood

The Esbat might be held in a building or in the open air. As a cottage room would be too small for thirteen people, the meeting was sometimes held in the church to the great scandal of all pious Christians. It was, however, more usual to meet in the open air and at no great distance from the village. Night was the ordinary time, but the meeting did not always last till dawn, it varied according to the amount of business to be transacted. Day Esbats are known, but these depended, as did all arrangements for an Esbat, on the will of the Master.

The Sabbaths were held quarterly, on the 2nd of February (Candlemas day), the Eve of May, the 1st of August (Lammas), and the Eve of November (All Hallow E'en). This shows a division of the year at May and November with two cross-quarter days. Such a division belongs to a very early calendar before the introduction of agriculture. It has no connection with sowing or reaping, it ignores the solstices and equinoxes, but it marks the opening of the two breeding seasons for animals, both wild and domesticated. It therefore belongs to the hunting and pastoral periods, and is in itself an indication of the extreme primitiveness of the cult and points to a very early origin, reaching back possibly to the Palaeolithic era. Cormac, archbishop of Cashel in the tenth century,[40] refers to these meetings when he says that 'in his time four great fires were lighted up on the four great festivals of the Druids, viz., in February, May, August, and November.' Seven centuries later, in 1661, Isobel Smyth of Forfar[41] acknowledged that 'by these meetings she met with him (i.e. the Devil) every quarter at Candlemas, Rood day, Lammas, and Hallowmass.' This shows the continuity of the Old Religion underlying the official religion of Christianity.

As the great Sabbaths were always held on the same dates every year no special notice was sent to summon the congregation. The site was always an open place, a moor or a hill-top, where numbers could be accommodated without difficulty. In France one of the places of assembly was the top of the Puy de Dôme, in Guernsey in the windswept neighbourhood of the dolmen known as the Catioroc; in England any open field or moor could be used, while in Scotland it was a moor or the sea-shore. The Sabbath began between nine and ten at night and the ceremonies ended at dawn, the crowing of the cocks indicating to a people who were innocent of watches and clocks, that the time of departure had come. At the spring festival the congregation appears to have returned to the village in a processional dance bringing in the May.

The regard which the members of the Old Religion had for the Sabbath is set forth by de Lancre, the French inquisitor, who was sent to exterminate the cult in the Pays de Labourd. Like all Christians he called these people 'witches', but at least he gives the very words they used. He examined two young women, one aged twenty-nine, the other twenty-eight. The former[42] said that 'the Sabbath was the true Paradise, where there was more joy than could be expressed. Those who went there found the time too short because of the pleasure and happiness they enjoyed, so that they left with infinite regret and longed for the time when they could go again.' The other young woman,[43] whom de Lancre appreciated as being very beautiful, 'deposed that she had a singular pleasure in going to the Sabbath, because the Devil so held their hearts and wills that he hardly allowed any other desire to enter therein. That she had more pleasure and happiness in going to the Sabbath than to Mass, for the Devil made them believe him to be the true God, and that the joy which the witches had at the Sabbath was but the prelude of much greater glory.' De Lancre records[44] that the witches 'said frankly that they who went had an over-powering desire (*désir enragé*) to go and to be there, finding the days before the so longed-for night so far off, and the hours required to get there so slow; and being there, too short for that delightful sojourn and delicious amusement.' Another French inquisitor, Jean Bodin, also notes the feeling of the 'witches' towards their religion, his record being

8a. EGYPTIAN JACKAL MASK

(ABOUT 600 B.C.)

8b. THE DORSET OOSER

9. A KNIGHT VISITING A FAIRY HOUSE

(*Olaus Magnus* 1555)

couched in the characteristically Christian manner of words, 'Satan promises that they shall be very happy after this life, which prevents their repenting, and they die obstinate in their wickedness.'[45]

An important part of a witch's outfit in popular estimation was a familiar. 'These witches have ordinarily a familiar or spirit in the shape of a Man, Woman, Boy, Dogge, Cat, Foale, Fowle, Hare, Rat, Toade, etc. And to these their spirits they give names, and they meet together to Christen them.'[46] An examination of the evidence shows that there were two kinds of familiar, one was for divining, the other for working magic. Familiars belonged apparently only to members of a coven, not to the congregation in general.

The divining familiar is co-terminous with the witch-religion. When a witch became a member of a coven she was told by what animal she should divine and was instructed in the method of divination. A very common animal for the purpose was a dog, sometimes though not always there was a restriction as to colour. Thus Elizabeth Style, in Somerset,[47] divined by a black dog, but Alse Gooderidge, in Derbyshire,[48] used a party-coloured dog belonging to a fellow-villager, to the great indignation of the dog's master. In sparsely populated districts where animals were scarce the witch might have more than one familiar. John Walsh, the Dorset witch,[49] divined by 'a blackish-gray culver or a brindled dog'; Alexander Hamilton in Lothian[50] had a crow, a cat and a dog as his divining animals; and Margaret Ningilbert, of Thurso, as late as 1719, divined by a black horse, a black cloud or a black hen.[51]

Her divining familiar was indicated to the witch by the Devil when she became a member of the coven, and she was instructed in the method of divining by that special animal. She could also have an animal of her own for private divination; these had to be named by a special ceremonial in which several members of the coven took part. The *Guide to Grand Jurymen* informs its readers that 'to these their spirits they give names, and they meet together to Christen them.' The

Lancashire witches met at Malkin Tower on Good Friday,[52] 'first was the naming of the Spirit, which Alizon Device, now Prisoner at Lancaster, had, but did not name him, because shee was not there.' The French evidence shows how these familiars could be used. Silvain Nevillon of Orleans, condemned to death in 1615,[53] said 'that there are witches who keep familiars (*marionettes*), which are little imps (*Diableteaux*) in the form of toads, and give them to eat a mess of milk and flour and give them the first morsel, and they do not dare to absent themselves from the house without asking leave, and they must say how long they will be absent, as three or four days; and if they (the familiars) say that it is too much those who keep them dare not make the journey or go against their will. And when they wish to go away on business or pleasure and to know if it will turn out well, they note if the familiars are joyous, in which case they go on business or pleasure; but if they are spiritless and sad, they do not budge from the house.' Gentien le Clerc, tried and condemned at the same time as Nevillon, declared that 'he had more trust in his familiar than in God, that there was more profit in it than in God, and that he gained nothing by looking to God, whereas his familiar always brought him something.'

The method of divination varied according to the animal used and according to the type of question asked. Agnes Sampson, executed 1590,[54] was accustomed to divine by a dog, when she was called in to see a sick person. When she was summoned to the bedside of a lady of high rank she went into the garden with the lady's daughters, and there she called 'Elva'. A large black dog appeared and she took the omens by its appearance and behaviour. It seems to have been a peculiarly savage animal and frightened the ladies by rushing at them and barking, and Sampson's prognostication was that the patient would die. This is the only detailed account of obtaining omens by animals as to the outcome of an illness. All methods of divination were as carefully taught to the witches as to the augurs of Rome. The Grandmaster appointed to each member the creature by which she would obtain the auguries and also the proper words to use before the animal appeared. The words always contained the name of the god. The whole method of augury seems to have been like the methods used in classical times.

The Domestic Familiar must on no account be confused with the Divining Familiar, with which it has little in common. The Divining Familiar was often a large creature, like a horse or a stag, or a large bird, like a crow or a wood-pigeon; if no animal or bird answered the call the auguries could be taken from a cloud. The essence of the Divining Familiar was that it was not an animal belonging to the witch, any creature of the required kind would be sufficiently good to draw omens from. The Divining Familiar was, as the name I have given to it implies, used only for prophetic purposes, and the use of divination by its means is almost universal. The Domestic Familiar was entirely different. It was always a small animal, which belonged to the witch, was kept in her house, and was often called an Imp or a Spirit, and occasionally a Devil, was fed in a special manner and was used only to carry out the commands of the witch. The geographical distribution of the domestic familiar suggests that it was in origin Scandinavian, Finnish or Lapp. A scientific study of the subject might throw light on some of the religious beliefs and practices of the early invaders of our eastern shores.

Originally the Domestic Familiar may have been in use in all parts of England. Bishop Hutchinson, who made a special study of witches, says, 'I meet with little mention of Imps in any Country but ours, where the Law makes the feeding, suckling or rewarding of them to be a felony.' The records of it, however, are almost entirely from the Eastern Counties, especially Essex and Suffolk. The accounts show that the custom of keeping and using these Familiars was very primitive, and may date back to the Palaeolithic period.

The Domestic Familiar was always a little creature—a little dog, a small cat, a rat, a mole, a toad, or a mouse—

which could be kept in the house in some small receptacle like a box or a pot. The creature was fed by its owner, originally that it might become tame and return to her after it had worked its magic. In the food was mixed a drop of the witch's blood so that the animal became in a sense a part of the owner. A name was always given to it, and in every way it was regarded as a creature of magical powers though under the control of its owner. It was used only for working magic, never for divining. This fact was known to the recorders. In 1587 Giffard states[55] that 'the witches have their spirits, some hath one, some hath more, as two, three foure, or five, some in one likenesse, and some in another, as like cats, weasils, toades, or mice, whom they nourish with milke or with a chicken, or by letting them suck now and then a drop of blood.' Though the Domestic Familiar was recognized theoretically in Scotland there is no mention of it in any Scotch witch-trial; it is found only in England, and there, with few exceptions, only on the east side.

Among the witches of Hatfield Peveril in Essex in 1556[56] Familiars could be hereditary and could also be presented. Elizabeth Francis was taught her religion by her grandmother, 'when she taught it her, she counselled her to renounce God and to give of her blood to Sathan (as she termed it) which she delivered to her in the likeness of a white spotted Cat.' Later on she went to her neighbour, Mother Waterhouse, 'she brought her this Cat in her apron and taught her as she was instructed by her grandmother, telling her that she must call him Sathan and give him of her blood and bread and milk as before.' Mother Waterhouse faithfully followed the instructions and 'gave him at all times when he did anything for her, by pricking her hand or face and putting the blood to his mouth which he sucked.' She was very poor and evidently found the cat too expensive to keep, and she confessed that 'she turned the cat into a toad by this means, she kept the cat a great while in wool in a pot, and at length being moved by poverty to occupy the wool, she prayed in the name of the Father, Son, and

Holy Ghost that it would turn into a toad, and forthwith it was turned into a toad, and so kept it in a pot without wool.' The feeding of a Familiar was clearly a ritual ceremony, for though Mother Waterhouse's evidence gives the ceremony most completely there are many other instances which show that when the creature had been used for magic it was given a drop of the witch's blood on its return. By degrees the accounts of the ceremony were more and more exaggerated by the recorders till they developed into stories of imps sucking the witches' blood. In the seventeenth century no witch-trial in the Eastern Counties was regarded as complete without full and lurid details of the witch and her Familiars.

In illustrations (Plate 12) the 'imps', though described as small dogs, cats, or other little creatures, are represented as monsters. That they were really ordinary animals is certain from the evidence given in many of the trials. Mother Waterhouse's account shows this clearly, and other Essex witches[57] gave the same kind of evidence. Thus Ursley Kemp in 1582 stated that 'she went unto Mother Bennet's house for a mess of milk, the which she had promised her. But at her coming this examinate saith that she knocked at her door, and no body made her any answer, whereupon she went to her chamber window and looked in thereat, saying, Ho, ho, mother Bennet, are you at home? And casting her eyes aside, she saw a spirit lift up a cloth lying over a pot, looking much like a ferret. And it being asked of this examinate why the spirit did look upon her, she said it was hungry.' Mother Bennet acknowledged to having Familiars, 'many times did they drink of her milk-bowl. And when, and as often as they did drink the milk, this Examinate saith that they went into the earthen pot, and lay in the wool.' Another witness stated at the Essex trials, that 'about the fourteenth or fifteenth day of January last she went to the house of William Hunt to see how his wife did, and she being from home she called at her chamber window and looked in, and then espied a spirit to look out of a potcharde from under a cloth, the nose thereof being brown like a ferret.' Elizabeth Sawyer, the

witch of Edmonton in 1621,[58] confessed that the Devil came
to her, 'he would come in the shape of a dog. When he came
barking to me he had then done the mischief that I bid him
to do for me. I did stroke him on the back, and then he
would beck unto me and wag his tail, as being therewith
content.'

Familiars could be bought and sold, for there is still extant
a record in the Manor Rolls of the Isle of Axholme of a man
complaining that he had paid threepence to another man for
a devil but had not yet received that for which he had paid.
The gift and use of a Familiar is recorded in the trial of
Frances Moore in 1646,[59] 'one goodwife Weed gave her a
white Cat, telling her that if she would deny God, and affirm
the same by her blood, then whomsoever she cursed and
sent that Cat unto, they should die shortly after.'

The Domestic Familiar also went by inheritance. Ales
Hunt and her sister Margerie Sammon of the same coven
as Mother Bennet and Ursley Kemp, deposed to having received their Familiars from their mother; Ales Hunt had
two spirits, one called Jack, the other Robbin; Margerie
Sammon 'hath also two spirits like Toades, the one called
Tom, and the other Robbyn; And saith further that she and
her said sister had the said spirits of their mother.'[57] Another
case of inheritance, which is one of the rare instances from
the west side of England, comes from Liverpool in 1667,[60]
'Margaret Loy, being arraigned for a witch, confessed that
she was one; and when she was asked how long she had so
been, replied, Since the death of her mother, who died thirty
years ago; and at her decease she had nothing to leave her
and this widow Bridge, that were sisters, but her two spirits;
and named them, the eldest spirit to this widow, and the
other spirit to her the said Margaret Loy.' Alse Gooderidge,
in Derbyshire, in 1597[61] confessed to having received her
Familiar in the same way, and there are other instances. The
inheritance of Familiars was known among the Pagan Lapps,
and is therefore an indication of the primitiveness of the
custom.

Another method, also primitive, of obtaining a Domestic Familiar, was to recite some form of words, and then to take as the Familiar the first small animal which appeared after the recitation. When the religion was organized the formula included the name of the Old God, or Devil as the Christian recorders called him. Joan Waterhouse, the eighteen-year-old daughter of the Mother Waterhouse mentioned above, wishing to injure a girl with whom she had quarrelled, 'did as she had seen her mother do, calling Sathan, which came to her (as she said) in the likeness of a great dog.'[56] And Elizabeth Sawyer, the witch of Edmonton,[58] said that 'the first time the Devil came to me was when I was cursing, swearing, and blaspheming.' If she were calling on the Old God the Christian recorders would naturally think her words were blasphemy.

It is very clear, then, that the Divining and the Domestic Familiars were entirely distinct. The Divining Familiar had to be indicated by the Grandmaster himself, and was never one particular animal, any animal of the class indicated by the Devil could be the Familiar for the time being; it did not usually belong to the witch, and it was used for foretelling the future, generally to forecast the result of an illness. The Domestic Familiar, on the other hand, could be presented by the Devil or by another witch, it could be inherited, it could be bought and sold, or it could come of its own accord, after the performance of some ritual action or the recitation of ritual words. It was always a small creature, which could be carried in the pocket or kept in the house in a box or pot, it was the absolute property of the owner, it had to be ritually fed, it was never used except for working magic and then only for carrying out a curse.

The Domestic Familiar came into such prominence during the trials of the Essex witches in 1645–6, owing to the sensational records of the two witch-finders, Matthew Hopkins and John Stearne, that it has ever since been regarded, though erroneously, as an essential part of the outfit of a witch.

The Priesthood

The Broom. In connection with the rites, more particularly with the processional dance, the broom plays a large part. To the modern reader the witch and her broom are so closely connected as to be almost one and the same. Modern pictures of witches show them flying through the air seated astride a broom, which is not the usual household implement but a besom of birch-twigs or of heather such as is now used only by gardeners. In the nursery rhyme of the *Old Woman tossed up in a Basket*, she does not ride on the broom, she carries it in her hand.

The connection in the popular mind between a woman and a broom probably took its rise in very early times, the explanation being that the broom is essentially an indoor implement, belonging therefore to the woman; the equivalent implement for a man is the pitchfork, which is for outdoor work only. This is the reason why, in medieval representations of witch-dances, the women or witches often hold brooms, while the men or devils carry pitchforks. The broom being so definitely a feminine tool came to be regarded as the symbol of a woman. Until within very recent times cottage-women in Surrey, when going out and leaving the house empty, put a broom up the chimney so that it was visible from the outside, in order to indicate to the neighbours that the woman of the house was from home. In other parts of England until the last century, a broom standing outside a door showed that the wife was absent and the husband at liberty to entertain his male friends. This identification of the woman and the broom is probably the true meaning of Isobel Gowdie's[62] statement that before leaving home to attend the Sabbath an Auldearne witch would place her broom on the bed to represent her to her husband, at the same time saying the words, 'I lay down this besom in the Devil's name; let it not stir till I come again.' The husband would then know that his wife had gone to her devotions.

The riding on a broom seems to be merely a variant of riding on some kind of stick. It appears to have been performed only by the members of a coven, and only for going to a Sabbath or for use in the processional dance. The sticks were stalks of the broom-plant, of ragwort, hemp, bean, or any hollow stalk; occasionally ash-branches were used, and in the Near East witches rode on palm-branches. It seems clear, then, that the act of riding, not the stick used, was the important part of the ceremony. In Europe, though the witches rode on the stems of various plants, there is little first-hand evidence of their flying through the air; the recorder has only 'heard tell' of such a feat.

In and before the sixteenth century the accounts of the means of locomotion to and from the Sabbath are reasonable. In 1592, Agnes Sampson acknowledged that she rode to the meeting at the church of North Berwick on a pillion behind her son-in-law, John Couper; the Lancashire witches were also horse-riders; and the Swedish witches rode to Blockula. This last is indicated by the evidence of a boy,[63] whose mistress wished him to go with her to the Sabbath, so he took his father's horse out of the field for the purpose; the animal was not sent back when the lady returned and the owner thought it lost, but found it again when the boy told him what had occurred. The rich Alsatian witches[64] went to the meetings in carriages or waggons; the poorer sort rode on sticks or walked. Usually when a witch claimed to have flown through the air to the Sabbath she had to acknowledge that by some untoward accident that means of conveyance failed and she had to return on foot. Silvain Nevillon, executed at Orleans in 1615, said that he 'went often to the Sabbath on foot being quite awake, and that he did not anoint (literally, grease) himself, as it was folly to grease oneself if one were not going far.'[65] Rather later in the seventeenth century the reports become more highly coloured, until in 1662, Isobel Gowdie[66] told the court that 'we take windle-straws or beanstalks and put them between our feet and say thrice, "Horse and hattock, Horse and go! Horse and pellatis, ho, ho!" and immediately we fly away wherever we would.'

One of the earliest references to the ritual riding of witches is in the Decree attributed to the Council of Ancyra in the ninth century.[67] The Decree does not mention that the witches flew through the air, but it states definitely that they rode on animals: 'Certain wicked women, reverting to Satan, and seduced by the illusion and phantoms of demons, believe and profess that they ride at night with Diana on certain beasts, with an innumerable multitude of women, passing over immense distances, obeying her commands as their mistress, and evoked by her on certain nights.' That such a Decree should have been made is proof that ritual riding was well known and considered a heathenish practice.

The first witch recorded to have been tried by the Church for her Faith was Dame Alice Kyteler, in 1324.[68] The lady owned a staff 'on which she ambled and galloped through thick and thin, when and in what manner she listed, after having greased it with the ointment which was found in her possession.' The ambling through thick and thin shows that the riding was on the ground, not in the air.

The riding on plant-stems by fairies was described by the poet Montgomerie in 1515 (see p. 46). The description shows that though the riders were mounted on bune-wands (i.e. hollow stalks), they did not fly in the air; on the contrary, they merely hobbled along, jumping (or hovand) up and down, perhaps to imitate the action of a horse, in the same way that Alice Kyteler 'ambled'. The witches of Lorraine, in 1589, went to the Sabbath[69] in family parties. Hensel Erich rode on a stick, his mother on a pitchfork, and his father on a great strong ox. The Inquisitor Boguet, in 1608,[70] says that the witches often went on foot to the assemblies, if the place were not far from their homes. 'Others go there, sometimes on a goat, sometimes on a horse, and sometimes on a broom (*balai*) or a rake, these last very often going out of the house by the chimney. These also rub themselves first with a certain grease or ointment; but the others do not rub themselves in any fashion.'

The earliest mention of a broom as a means of locomotion

is in the trial of Guillaume Edelin, Prior of Saint-Germain-en-Laye, in 1453.[71] He confessed to having gone to the Sabbath mounted on a *balai*. In 1563 Martin Tulouff, of Guernsey,[72] declared that he saw his old witch-mother seat herself on a *genest* and ride up the chimney on it, saying as she mounted, 'Go, in the name of the Devil and Lucifer, over rocks and thorns.' In 1598 the French witch, Françoise Secretain,[73] went to the assembly on a white stick which she put between her legs; and in 1603 the Belgian witch, Claire Goessen,[74] was transported to the place of meeting on a stick smeared with ointment. The general evidence points to the conclusion that the ritual riding was not performed by the ordinary members of the congregation but was confined to the covens or priesthood.

The use of oil or ointment to facilitate the riding is mentioned by all the contemporary writers on the subject. It would seem that in early times the stick itself was greased, later it was the rider who was anointed. A form of magical words was also used when starting. According to de Lancre[75] the Basque witches 'when they anoint themselves, say "Emen hetan, Emen hetan", *Here and there, Here and there*. Others say, "I am the Devil. I have nothing which is not thine. In thy name, Lord, this thy servant anoints herself, and should be some day Devil and Evil Spirit like thee." '

In another part of France in 1652[76] a witch confessed that 'when she wished to go to the dances, she anointed herself with an ointment given to her by a man-witch, who was sent by the Devil.' The Somerset witches[77] averred in 1664 that 'they anoint their Foreheads and Handwrists with an oil the Spirit brings them (which smells raw) and then they are carried in a very short time, using these words as they pass, *Thout, tout a tout, tout, throughout and about*.' The Swedish witches in 1670[78] stated that Antecessor, as they called their god, 'gives us a horn with a salve in it, wherewith we anoint ourselves, whereupon we call upon the Devil and away we go.'

Several recipes for flying ointments are extant. Professor

The Priesthood

A. J. Clark[79] has reported on three, and shows that aconite and belladonna are among the ingredients; aconite produces irregular action of the heart and belladonna causes delirium. 'Irregular action of the heart in a person falling asleep produces the well-known sensation of suddenly falling through space, and it seems quite possible that the combination of a delirifacient like belladonna with a drug producing irregular action of the heart like aconite might produce the sensation of flying.' It seems therefore that it was immaterial whether the stick or the rider were anointed; sooner or later the sensation of flying would be felt and the rider would be convinced that she had flown through the air.

The original broom, whether for domestic or magical purposes, was a stalk of the broom plant with a tuft of leaves at the end. The number of beliefs and proverbial sayings connected with the plant show that it was supposed to possess magical qualities. These qualities had to do with the giving and blasting of fertility. A broomstick marriage was not uncommon in periods when marriage laws were not very strict; it was not always considered binding by the Christians who practised it. Jumping over the broomstick is said to have formed part of the gypsy marriage rites. On the other hand there is still the old saying in use in some parts of England, which indicates that the broom-plant had blasting qualities, 'If you sweep the house with blossomed broom in May, you will sweep the head of the house away.'

The most important example of a processional broom survives in the Prize Besom of Shaftesbury. A description of it occurs in an agreement made in 1662 between the Mayor and Corporation of Shaftesbury and Sir Edward Nicholas, in which the Burgesses of the town ask that the annual procession in May should not take place on a Sunday. 'The said Mayor, accompanied with some of the Burgesses and other Inhabitants of the said Town and Borough, have used to walk out into a Place called Enmore-Green, where is a Pool of Water, and divers Springs and Wells; and in that Place, to walk or dance Hand in Hand round the same Green

92

in a long Dance, there being a Musician or Tabor and Pipe, and also a Staffe or Besome adorned with Feathers, Pieces of Gold, Rings and other Jewells, called a Prize Besom' (Plate 13). A description of the long dance mentioned in this quotation is given on p. 108.

The importance of the broom in India is as great as in Europe, but as the sweepers belong to one of the lowest castes it is difficult to obtain much information. One 'sect' is known as *Mehtars*; a word which means prince or leader, a Mehtar is therefore often addressed as Maharaj. The ordinary house-broom is made of date-palm leaves and is considered sacred, but it has not the magical qualities of the sweeper's broom which is made of split bamboo. 'It is a powerful agent for curing the evil eye, and mothers get the sweeper to come and wave it up and down in front of a sick child for this purpose.'[80] The dead of the sweeper-caste are buried face downwards to prevent the spirit from escaping, for a sweeper's ghost is regarded as extremely malevolent; this custom should be compared with the burial of a witch at the cross-roads with a stake through her heart, which was done to prevent the ghost from walking. In some places the sweepers carry a decorated broom in procession at the festival of their god, Lal-beg.

The Rites

The ceremonies of the cult are fully recorded in the trials of the 'witches' in all parts of Europe. These ceremonies comprise the rites of admission, sacred dances, feasts, and orgiastic rites, besides other ceremonies which to our minds are more purely religious, such as homage to the god, sacrifices, prayers and the like.

Admission Ceremonies. In all organized religions there is some form of admission into the cult by which a candidate can become a member. Often there are two forms, the first when a young infant is received, the other when at puberty the candidate takes on himself the full membership. For an adult convert the two ceremonies are combined with the necessary modifications. In these respects the Witch-religion, i.e. the cult of the Horned God, conforms to the ordinary routine of all religions.

The form for the admission of infants is best recorded in France.[1] The mother took her young child to one of the great quarterly Sabbaths, and kneeling before the Incarnate God she said, 'Great Lord, whom I worship, I bring thee a new servant who will be thy slave for ever.' At a sign from the god she moved forward on her knees and laid the infant in the divine arms. Such a ceremony, at once simple and touching, must have had a great effect on the minds of the mothers; they saw with their own eyes that the god himself had received the child. In some places the infant was also baptized with water, and at Orleans chrism was used.[2]

All the inquisitors and other recorders mention that the

'witches' were exceedingly careful to have their children received by their god, and to bring them up in the tenets and practice of the Pagan religion. Such an attitude of mind would have brought nothing but praise had the parents been of the same religion as the recorders and judges, but as the parents belonged to another faith their action in the matter was regarded as essentially wicked. The French inquisitors were peculiarly horrified at the numbers of children dedicated to the non-Christian deity, 'witches were accustomed to have their children baptized more often at the Sabbath than in church, and presented more often to the Devil than to God.'[3] In 1578 Jeanne Hervillier,[4] who was from Verberie, near Compiègne, deposed that from her birth she was dedicated to the Devil by her mother. Boguet[5] in 1598 relates that Pierre Willermoz, being only ten years old, was taken by his father to the Sabbath, and that three other very young children were taken in the same way by their maternal grandmother. In the Home for poor girls founded by Madame Bourignon at Lille, one of the girls told Madame Bourignon[6] in 1661 that 'her mother had taken her with her when she was very young and had even carried her in her arms to the Witches' Sabbath.' Another girl, still younger, had been a constant attendant at the Sabbath since she was a little child. Madame Bourignon, who was a deeply religious Christian, was shocked at the ignorance of Christianity displayed by the girls under her care, and records that they were 'for the most part so ignorant of the fact of their salvation that they lived like animals.'

If in the course of a trial it transpired that an accused had been thus dedicated in infancy it was proof positive that he or she came of a witch family, which was in itself such strong presumptive evidence of witch propensities that few, if any, escaped after the fact came to light. Reginald Scot[7] is very definite on this point; quoting from Bodin he says, 'Witches must be examined, whether their parents were witches or no, for witches come by propagation.' In another place[8] he quotes from Cornelius Agrippa that 'in Brabant a woman was accused as a witch and one of the proofs against her was that her mother was in times past burned for a witch.'[6] Jeanne Hervillier's mother[9] was burnt as a witch long before Jeanne herself was accused. One of the strong proofs of witchcraft against Elizabeth Clarke in Essex in 1645[10] was that her mother and some other of her kinsfolk 'did suffer death for witchcraft and murder.' The mother and aunt of Alexander Sussums of Melford, in Suffolk, in 1645[11] were both hanged and his grandmother burnt for being witches; 'so others of them questioned and hanged.' Everywhere the 'witch-brood' received scant mercy at the hands of the authorities.

When the child was old enough to understand, an age which varied from nine to thirteen years, he made a public profession of faith.[12] This was not necessarily at a great Sabbath, but had to be done before witnesses. The candidate prostrated himself on the ground at the feet of the Divine Man who asked, 'Dost thou come of thy own free will?' The candidate replied, 'Yes'. The god then said, 'Do what I desire and what I do.' The candidate still kneeling made the profession of faith, 'Thou art my god and I am thy slave.' Homage was then rendered to the god, and the novice was marked[13] on some part of the person so that he might be known by others as a full member. The mark was either a scar or a tattoo. These ceremonies are paralleled in modern times among many races, the physical mark being often an essential part of the proceedings. Madame Bourignon says,[14] 'When a child offered to the Devil by its Parents, comes to the use of Reason, the Devil then demands its soul and makes it deny God and renounce its Baptism, and all relating to the Faith, promising Homage and Fealty to the Devil in manner of a Marriage, and instead of a Ring, the Devil gives them a Mark with an iron Awl in some part of the Body.' Bodin notes[15] that 'fathers and mothers consecrate and dedicate their children to the Devils, some when they are newly born, others while still unborn. The Devils do not make express paction with the children vowed to them until

10. DANCE OF WOMEN

Palaeolithic Painting at Cogul

11. ROBIN GOODFELLOW

they reach the age of puberty.' Elizabeth Francis, tried at Chelmsford[16] in 1556, was taught 'the art of witchcraft', i.e. her religion, by her grandmother when she reached the age of twelve. Elizabeth Demdike,[17] the most celebrated of all the Lancashire witches, 'brought up her own children, instructed her grandchildren, and took great care and pains to bring them to be Witches.' Had Elizabeth Demdike been a Christian she would have been held up to admiration as a pattern of what a pious and devout woman should be. At Paisley, Annabil Stuart[18] was fourteen when at her mother's instance she made the vows to the Devil. In this connection it may be noted that Joan of Arc was twelve years old when she first began to take an active part in her religion, and that much of her religious instruction came from the godmother who had dealings with the fairies.

The rites for the admission of an adult convert were more dramatic than those for a boy or girl already belonging to the religion. The accounts are fuller as the records were made when the cult of the Horned God was already waning and had to keep up its numbers by proselytizing. As in all admissions to a new religion the convert had to renounce his old faith, and this renunciation was made as explicit as possible. 'I renounce and deny God, the blessed Virgin, the Saints, baptism, father, mother, relations, heaven, earth, and all that is in the world,'[19] was one of several formulae; which always had to be 'an express renunciation of Jesus Christ and of the Faith.' Then came the baptism, the profession of faith and the vow of fidelity,[20] 'I place myself at every point in thy power and in thy hands, recognizing no other god, for thou art my god.' A variant of the vow of fidelity much used in Scotland[21] was that the candidate placed one hand on the crown of her head, the other under the sole of her foot, and dedicated all that was between the two hands to the service of her god. The solemn vow of self-dedication to the deity actually present in person must have been peculiarly impressive. The Swedish witches[22] had a special rite which was obviously intended to impress ignorant minds.

They were given a little bag containing a few shavings of a clock to which a stone was tied; they threw this into the water, saying, 'As these shavings of the clock do never return to the clock from which they are taken, so may my soul never return to heaven.' This renunciation of a previous religion is noted as early as 1584 by Reginald Scot,[23] who was one of the first to raise his voice against the persecution by Christians of the heathen in their midst, 'As our witches are said to renounce Christ and despite his sacraments: so doo the other forsake Mahomet and his lawes.'

After the renunciation of his old religion the convert advanced to the actual admission ceremony, which consisted of baptism and marking. Baptism was the less important part in the eyes of the members of the cult and was often omitted. It was, however, a rite which was in force before the introduction of Christianity and has therefore a definite bearing on the antiquity of the religion of the Horned God. Adult baptism, as recorded in the New Testament, was apparently performed by immersion in a river, but the witch-baptism varied from dipping the head in water to a mere sprinkling; total immersion is never recorded. The rite must have been general throughout western and central Europe, as Sir George Mackenzie[24] quotes Delrio to the effect that 'the Devil useth to Baptize them of new, and to wipe off their Brow their old Baptism.' In France baptism of children only is noted, and it is a remarkable fact that baptism either of adults or children is never mentioned in English trials though it is recorded in New England. Adult baptism is found in the accounts from Scotland and Sweden. The earliest is from Bute in 1669,[25] when several witches gave evidence; Margret NcLevine said, 'He asked, what was her name. She answered him, Margret, the name that God gave me, and he said to her, I baptize thee Jonet'; Isobel NcNicoll confessed that 'he baptized her and gave her a new name and called her Caterine'; Jonet NcNicoll 'confesses with remorse' that she met 'a gross copper-faced man, whom she knew to be an evil spirit, and that he gave her a new name, saying, I baptize thee Mary'; Jonet Morisoun 'trysted with the Devil, and he asked what was her name, and she answered, Jonet Morisoun, the name that God gave me, and he said, believe not in Christ but believe in me. I baptize thee Margaret.' In Sweden[26] the converts had to make an oath of fidelity on the occasion of the baptism, 'he caused them to be baptized by such Priests as he had there, and made them confirm their Baptism with dreadful Oaths and Imprecations.' The 'oaths and imprecations' are recorded by Boguet[27] in a more reasonable manner, 'He makes them give up their part in Paradise' [i.e the Christian heaven], 'and makes them promise that they will hold him as their sole master for ever, and that they will always be faithful to him. Above all, he makes them swear very solemnly that they will never accuse one another, nor report anything which has passed among them.' In New England[28] baptism is recorded as being practised regularly. Mary Osgood said that 'she was baptized by the Devil, who dipped her face in the water, and made her renounce her former baptism, and told her she must be his, soul and body, for ever and ever.' Goody Lacey[29] saw six baptized, 'he dipped their heads in the water, saying, they were his.'

The kiss often followed the baptism. The new member kissed the Grandmaster on any part of his person that he directed. This was in token of absolute subjection, such as was found in the Middle Ages in the kissing of the Pope's foot or the kissing of the hand of a monarch. The recorders, however, disregarded the Christian parallels, and make a great feature of the kiss as being most humiliating.

The marking of the new convert was another ceremony which appealed to the imagination of the recorders, and is therefore described in some detail. *The Mysterie of Witch-craft*,[30] written in 1617, tells us that 'the Devil sets his seale upon them. This is commonly some sure marke in some secret place of their bodies, which shall remain sore and un-healed until his next meeting with them, and then for after-wards prove ever insensible.' The author of *The Lawes against* *Witches and Conjuration*, published 'By Authority' in 1645, states that 'the Devil leaveth markes upon their bodies, sometimes like a Blew-spot, or a Red-spot like a flea-biting.' Sir George Mackenzie,[31] the great Scotch lawyer, writing on the legal aspect of the subject, says, 'The Devil's Mark useth to be a great Article with us, but it is not *per se* found relevant, except it be confest by them, that they got that Mark with their own consent; *quo casu*, it is equivalent to a paction. The Mark is given to them, as is alledg'd, by a Nip in any part of the body, and it is blew.'

The evidence shows that the mark was caused by pricking or cutting the skin till blood came; the operator then passed his hand over the wound, there was a considerable amount of pain which lasted some days or even longer; when the wound healed the resultant red or blue mark was indelible. This process is obviously some form of tattooing, and is perhaps the attenuated survival of the ancient British and Pictish custom of tattooing the whole body with blue pigment, a custom which among the witches was not confined to Great Britain, but extended to the Continent as well, particularly to France.

There was no special place on the body on which the mark was made, though Boguet says that it was usually on the left shoulder.[32] De Lancre[33] says that in his part of the country the left side and the left shoulder were marked, that the skin was torn to the effusion of blood, and that the pain might last for three months. He also says that there was a sensation of heat which penetrated into the flesh. Jeanne d'Abadie[34] told de Lancre that when the Devil marked her on the right shoulder he hurt her so much that she cried out, and felt at the time a great heat as if a fire had burned her. The marking of witches in other countries was not so dramatically recorded. The Belgian witch, Elisabeth Vlamynx,[35] tried in 1595, merely stated that she was marked on the left armpit. Two witches tried at Aberdeen[36] in 1597 confessed to the Devil's marks, Andro Man that 'Christsonday bit a mark in the third finger of thy right hand, which thou hast yet to show', and Christian Mitchell that 'the Devil gave thee a nip on the back of thy right hand, for a mark that thou was one of his number.' Sylvine de la Plaine,[37] a young married woman aged twenty-three, confessed at Brécy in 1616 that she had been marked on the crown of the head and on the right thigh. The Yarmouth[38] witch, tried in 1644, saw a tall black man at her door, 'he told her he must see her Hand; and then taking out something like a Pen-knife, he gave it *a little Scratch* so that Blood followed, and the *Mark* remained to that time.' The Essex witch, Rebecca Jones,[39] told the magistrates that a handsome young man came to the door whom 'now she thinks was the devil; who asked this examinate how she did and desired to see her left wrist, which she showed unto him; and he then took a pin from this examinant's own sleeve, and pricked her wrist twice, and there came out a drop of blood, which he took off with the top of his finger, and so departed.' The Forfar witches,[40] tried in 1661, were marked on the shoulder, Jonet Howat said that 'the devil nipped her upon one of her shoulders, so as she had great pain for some time thereafter', that when he came again he 'stroked her shoulder (which he had nipped) with his hand, and that presently after she was eased of her former pain.' Another witch of the same coven was also nipped in the same way; four weeks later 'the devil stroked her shoulder with his fingers, and after that she had ease in the place formerly nipped by the Devil.' Marie Lamont of Innerkip,[41] in 1662, stated that 'the Devil nipped her on the right side which was very painful for a time, but thereafter he stroked it with his hand, and healed it; this she confesses to be his mark.' In Bute[42] in 1662, Margaret NcWilliam, who seems to have been one of the chief witches there, was marked in three places, one near her left shinbone, another between her shoulders, and the third on the hip, all of them blue marks. Margret NcLevine, of the same coven, stated that the Devil came to her, 'he took her by the middle finger of the right hand which he had almost cut off her, and therewith left her. Her finger was so sorely pained for the space of a month thereafter that there was no pain comparable to it, as also took her by the right leg which was sorely pained likewise as also by the Devil.' Three of the Wincanton witches[43] were found to be marked at their trial in 1664; 'he prickt the fourth Finger of Elizabeth Style's right hand between the middle and upper joynt (where the sign at the Examination remained)'; in the case of Alice Duke, 'he prickt the fourth finger of her right hand between the middle and upper joynt (where the mark is yet to be seen)'; and in the case of Christian Green, 'the Man in Black prickt the fourth finger of her Right hand between the middle and upper joints, where the sign yet remains.' Annabil Stuart of Paisley,[44] who was only fourteen when tried in 1678, said that 'the Devil took her by the Hand and nipped her Arm, which continued to be sore for half an hour.' At Borrowstowness, in 1679, Margaret Pringle[45] stated that the Devil took her by the right hand, 'whereby it was grievously pained; but having it touched of new again, it immediately became whole.' Little Thomas Lindsay, of Renfrewshire,[46] when he joined the coven, had 'a Nip on the Neck, which continued sore for Ten days'; and John Reid, who later suffered the traitor's death in prison, received 'a Bite or Nipp in his Loyn, which he found painfull for a Fortnight.' Isobel Adams of Pittenweem, said at her trial in 1704, that 'the Devil put his mark in her flesh which was very painful.'[47] In 1705 the two Northampton witches,[48] Elinor Shaw and Mary Phillips, who like the rest of that coven remained faithful to their god unto death, had been pricked at their finger ends.

The Pact or Covenant was probably a late custom, introduced when the religion was falling into decay. In all religions the god promises to the convert eternal life and eternal happiness in return for fidelity and service, but the promise of mundane help enforced by a written contract suggests a form of propaganda which could only have occurred when the religion was hard pressed for converts. The written contract was the most important part of the admission ceremony in the eyes of the legal authorities who tried the witches; it appeared to give an air of finality to the whole transaction. Occasionally, especially in France, one of these written covenants fell into the hands of the inquisitors, unfortunately the exact wording is never given in the records, the inquisitor preferring to make his readers' flesh creep by saying that 'it was so horrible that one had horror in seeing it.'[49] In England and Scotland there is no record of such a contract having been brought into court as evidence against an accused person; it would appear that the Devil kept the paper in some secure place and perhaps destroyed it if there were danger.

No contract was signed without the free consent of the contracting parties, as is clearly shown in many of the trials; the Devil always asked the candidate whether he or she wished to become his servant and the paper was not produced unless the answer was very definitely in the affirmative. If the witch could not write she signed the paper with a cross or circle, or the Devil put his hand on hers and guided her hand in signing her name. The signing is usually said to have been done with the blood of the witch drawn from some part of her person for the purpose; this is, however, merely a confusion with the marking of the candidate when the skin was cut to the effusion of blood. In the later rite, the blood was a convenient fluid for writing the signature when ink was a rare commodity, as is always the case in country places. It is possible also that the blood thus drawn may have been regarded as an offering to the new god. The contract was originally made out and signed on a separate piece of parchment or paper; in the later trials it was said to be in a book, but this is probably a confusion with the Devil's book in which the records were made at the Sabbaths. In America the book was constantly mentioned by the parsons and ministers who recorded the trials. Forbes, in his *Institutes of the Law of Scotland*, says, 'An express Covenant is entered into betwixt a Witch and the Devil appearing in some visible Shape. Whereby the former renounceth God and His

Baptism, engages to serve the Devil, and do all the Mischief he can as Occasion offers, and leaves his Soul and Body to his Disposal after Death. The Devil on his Part articles with such Proselytes concerning the Shape he is to appear to them in, the Services they are to expect from him, upon the Performance of certain Charms or ceremonious Rites.' Claire Goessen,[50] a Belgian witch tried in 1603, made a covenant with the Devil, 'this pact was written on paper by Satan himself with blood taken from a prick which she made for that purpose with a pin in the thumb of her left hand, and was signed by the prisoner with her own blood.' Half a century later, in 1657, a Belgian man-witch named Mathieu Stoop, signed a pact with blood drawn from his right leg, but was marked at the same time in the right armpit.

Various methods of making a pact with the Devil were in vogue in France, Belgium and Wales until a recent period. In Belgium[51] the would-be candidate goes to a cross-road at night carrying a black hen. The Devil in the form of a man will come and bargain for the hen, then will buy it by giving the seller what he desires. The pact is made for the duration of seven years. In the Department of Entre-Sambre-et-Meuse,[52] the ritual is slightly different: 'Come to the wood and you will see a man coming to you. This is the chief. He will ask if you will engage in his society. If you refuse he will tell you to return whence you came. If you accept, the term of the engagement is for seven years, and you will get a *plaquette* a day.' The Welsh method carries on the idea of the magical power of the Host. In North Pembrokeshire[53] an old man-witch gave an account of how he obtained his power. When he went to his first Communion he made pretence of eating the bread 'and then put it in his pocket. When he went forth from the service there was a dog meeting him by the gate, to which he gave the bread, thus selling his soul to the Devil. Ever after, he possessed the power to bewitch.'

The contract between the Devil and the witch was generally for the term of the witch's life, but contracts for a term of years are often found. Records and tradition agree in stating that the number of years was seven, though there is some evidence that nine years was also a favourite number. At the end of the term the witch was at liberty to refuse to renew it. The length of the term suggests that it was connected with the cycle of years for the Great Sacrifice in which the god himself was the Divine Victim. If this theory is correct it means that the witch was the substitute for the god, and explains why in so many cases the Devil promised that she should have power and riches during the interval before the end came. In all records of the substitute for the Divine Victim the mock king is allowed the royal power for a certain length of time before the sacrifice is consummated. This I take to be the meaning of the numerous stories of persons selling their souls for the sake of being rich for a term of years and being killed by the Devil at the end of that term.

As might be expected in an organized and devout community, marriage was regarded as a religious ceremony and was therefore solemnized at the Sabbath by the god himself. These were the everyday permanent marriages of an ordinary village, and show how the cult permeated the whole religious organization and life of the people. Gaule[54] makes the general statement that the Devil 'oft-times marries them ere they part, either to himselfe, or their Familiar, or to one another; and that by the Book of Common Prayer.' De Lancre[55] is very explicit, 'The Devil performs marriages at the Sabbath between male and female witches. Joining their hands he says to them aloud: *Esta es buena parati, Esta parati lo toma.*' In Lorraine[56] Agnes Theobalda said that she was at the wedding when Cathalina and Engel von Hudlingen took their Beelzebubs in marriage. In Sweden[57] 'the Devil had Sons and Daughters whom he did marry together.' Besides the permanent unions there were temporary marriages in which the ceremonies were equally solemn; Gaule has confused the two kinds in his account. Such witch-marriages occurred in many places but they are more fully recorded in Lorraine than elsewhere. Sometimes one, sometimes both, of the contracting parties were already married to other partners, but that did not appear to be an obstacle, and the wedding gave an extra and special reason for feasting and joyousness.

Dances. At the meetings, both Sabbaths and Esbats, the proceedings often began and terminated with dancing, and in the dances the connection between the witches and the fairies is clearly seen. In all serious accounts of the fairies they are recorded as taking part in two important ceremonies in public; one is the procession, the other is the round dance. The dates of these ceremonies are the four great quarterly festivals, more particularly May-day and All Hallow E'en.

The origin of these ceremonies was undoubtedly religious, and they were in all probability derived from some form of imitative magic. When any ceremony is performed by several people together it tends to become rhythmic, and a dance is evolved in which, after a time, the actions are so conventionalized as to be almost unrecognizable. The so-called Fertility Dances are a case in point, for though they were once common throughout the world they survive in recognizable form only among the more backward peoples. In Europe the details have not always been preserved, and it is often solely by comparison with the dances of savages that their original meaning can be seen. In Crete the dance of Ariadne, performed by youths and maidens, belonged apparently to the Fertility group, so also did the processional dance of the Bacchantes. Mars in Rome was served by dancing priests, and the running step with which Moslems go round the Ka'aba is perhaps the survival of a sacred dance at Mecca.

The processional dance might be performed either on foot or on horseback, the essential part being that there was a leader, whose course was followed and whose actions were imitated by the rest of the dancers. The procession of the fairies was always on horseback, but the Bacchae of ancient times and the medieval witches danced the processional dance on foot. The round dance, whether of witches or fairies, was also on foot. The dancing ground was regarded as sacred, and often the dancers assembled in the village and danced their way to the holy spot. A survival of such a processional dance is seen in the folk-dance known as 'Green Garters', which carried the procession from the place of assembling to the Maypole, and was throughout England the customary introduction to the Maypole rites (Plate 14*b*).

A fact which stamps the processional dance as a religious rite is that it was often danced in the churchyard. To quote only a few out of many examples, in 1282[58] the priest of Inverkeithing 'led the ring' in his own churchyard, the dancers being his own parishioners. The quaint old story of the *Sacrilegious Carollers*[59] tells of a company of thirteen persons of both sexes, of whom the chief was the priest's daughter, who danced in a churchyard; this was in 1303 (Plate 14*b*). In 1590, Barbara Napier[60] met the covens of North Berwick at the church, 'where she danced endlong the kirkyard, and Gelie Duncan played on a trump, John Fian masked led the ring, Agnes Sampson and her daughters and all the rest following the said Barbara to the number of seven score persons.' The religious importance of the churchyard dances caused them to survive long after the Middle Ages. Aubrey[61] notes that in Herefordshire the village lads and lasses danced in the churchyards on all holydays and the eves of holydays; in Wales,[62] too, the same custom was kept up till late in the nineteenth century, but there the dancing was always confined to the north side of the churchyard where burials are fewest.

One of the most surprising survivals of the processional dance was to be found at Shaftesbury. Like 'Green Garters' it was connected with the May-day ceremonies, showing that it was in origin essentially religious. The petition of the civic authorities in the reign of Charles II is still extant, praying that the date of the dance might be changed from Sunday to a week-day, as the performance interfered with the attendance at church. This shows that the sanctity of the dance was such that it had to be performed on the sacred day. The description of the dance as seen by an eye-witness is published in the *Sporting Magazine* for 1803.

The Rites

'The inhabitants of Shaftesbury have an annual custom of great singularity called the Besant, or a May Day Dance for the Waters of Mottcomb. The last new married couple of the town come in the morning to the Mayor's House and are presented, the one with a fine Holland Shirt, the other with a Shift of the same material, elegantly adorned with ribbons of all the colours of the Rainbow. With these begin the procession, and immediately after them a party bearing a large dish, in which is placed a calf's head, with a purse of money in the mouth. Round the buds or young horns is wreathed a chaplet composed of all the flowers of the season. Over this the Besant* is held at the end of a pole by a man dressed in singular uniform. Now comes the Mayor and his Aldermanic body; at the sound of the music, of which there is great plenty, the whole are put in motion, youth, age and even decrepitude, begin to dance, and in this way quit the town, descend the hill, and never cease leaping and prancing till they arrive at the Well of Mottcomb where the owners of the water wait to receive their merry customers. After a short speech of ceremony, the Mayor presents the Besant to buy the waters for another year; and now Mr. Mayor, unwilling to leave so valuable a pledge behind, begins to treat for a redemption, when the Foreman of the Mottcomb people consents for the whole. Having received the dish with the calf's head, the purse of money and a new pair of laced gloves, he returns the Besant to the Magistrate, who having refreshed himself and Company on Mottcomb Green, return dancing in the most ridiculous way to the place from whence they came, finishing the day with May Games and the greatest Festivity' (see Plate 13).

The survivals of the processional dance in modern times are the Furry dance of England and the Farandole of France. In both these dances the performers hold hands to form a chain, and wind in and out of every room in every house of the village; where the leader goes the others must go, what

*For the description of the Besant or Byzant, see under Broom, p. 92.

the leader does the others must do. The dancers of the Farandole must be unmarried; and as the dance is often performed at night they either carry lanterns or 'wear a round of waxen tapers on the head' like the fairies (Plate 15). According to Jeanne Boisdeau,[63] in 1594, the dance at the top of the Puy de Dôme was danced back to back and was led by a great black goat, the oldest person present followed directly after him holding to his tail, and the rest came after holding hands. This seems to have been a circular dance to begin with, followed by a dancing procession. The Follow-my-leader dance was always of great importance among the witches, and it was essential that the leader should be young and active as pace was required. At Auldearne,[64] in 1662, the Maiden of the Coven was nicknamed 'Over the dyke with it', because as Isobel Gowdie explained, 'the Devil always takes the Maiden in his hand next him when we would dance Gillatrypes; and when he would leap from' [the words are broken here] 'he and she will say "Over the dyke with it".' At Aberdeen,[65] Thomas Leyis was the leader and knocked down a certain Kathren Mitchell, 'because she spoiled your dance, and ran not so fast about as the rest.' At Crighton,[66] Mr. Gideon Penman 'was in the rear in all their dances and beat up those that were slow.'

As the processional dance was performed by men and women side by side in pairs or in a long line with the sexes alternately, it was liable to break up into couples who continued dancing together after the procession was ended. Reginald Scot[67] says a dance of this kind was called *La Volta*, an interesting piece of information for La Volta is said to be the origin of the modern waltz.

The processional dance could be in itself a complete act of worship, but it was most frequently used to bring the worshippers to the holy place where the round dance or 'Ring' was to be performed.

The ring dance was specially connected with the fairies, who were reported to move in a ring holding hands. It is the earliest known dance, for there is a representation of one

at Cogul in north-eastern Spain (Catalonia), which dates to
the Late Palaeolithic or Capsian period (Plate 10). The dancers are all women, and their peaked hoods, long breasts,
and elf-locks should be noted and compared with the pictures
and descriptions of elves and fairies. They are apparently
dancing round a small male figure who stands in the middle.
A similar dance was performed and represented several
thousand years later, with Robin Goodfellow in the centre
of the ring and his worshippers forming a moving circle
round him (Plate 11). Though the interval of time between
the two representations is very great it is obvious that the
ceremony is the same in both cases, but the later example is,
as might be expected, more detailed and sophisticated. The
central figure is bearded like the Dancing God of Ariège,
but the animal's skin has degenerated into animal's legs.
The number of performers in the Robin Goodfellow picture
is thirteen, including the god and the musician; there are
only nine in the Cogul painting; but in both the Palaeolithic
and medieval examples the dancers are as carefully hatted
or hooded as any fairy.

Other sacred dances were known in ancient times. The
Therapeutae, at the beginning of the Christian era, had a
religious service very like that of the witches: 'After the feast
they celebrate the sacred festival during the whole night.
They sing hymns in honour of God, at one time all singing
together, and at another moving their hands and dancing in
corresponding harmony. Then when each chorus of the men
and each chorus of the women has feasted by itself separately,
like persons in the Bacchanalian revels, they join together.'[68]
This is so like the singing dances of the witches that it is
possible that both derive from the same source. Yet no one
accuses the Therapeutae of sorcery or devil-worship, for our
knowledge of them comes from a sympathetic recorder.

Another singing dance, also of moderate antiquity though
within the Christian era, is that attributed to Christ and the
disciples.[69] The date is not accurately known, but part of
the chant is quoted by Augustine (died A.D.430) in the

Epistle to Ceretius, and part of sections 93–5 and 97–8 were read at the Second Nicene Council. The whole chant is too long to transcribe here, I therefore quote only a few lines.

(94) 'Now before he was taken by the lawless Jews he gathered all of us together and said: Before I am delivered up unto them let us sing an hymn to the Father, and so go forth to that which lieth before us. He bade us therefore make as it were a ring, holding one another's hands, and himself standing in the midst he said: Answer Amen unto me. He began, then, to sing an hymn and to say: Glory be to thee, Father. And we, going about in a ring, answered him: Amen. (95) I would be saved, and I would save. Amen. I would be washed, and I would wash. Amen. Grace danceth; I would pipe; dance ye all. Amen. I would mourn; lament ye all. Amen. The number Eight (*lit*: one ogdoad) singeth praise with us. Amen. The number Twelve danceth on high. Amen. The Whole on high hath part in our dancing. Amen. Whoso danceth not, knoweth not what cometh to pass. Amen. I would flee, and I would stay. Amen. (96) Now answer thou unto my dancing. Behold thyself in me who speak, and seeing what I do, keep silence about my mysteries. Thou that dancest, perceive what I do, for thine is this passion of the manhood, which I am about to suffer. Thy god am I, not the god of the traitor. I would keep tune with holy souls. I have leaped; but do thou understand the whole, and having understood it, say: Glory be to the Father. Amen. (97) Thus, my beloved, having danced with us the Lord went forth.' The early date of this singing dance shows the importance attached to this mode of worship, which though heathen in origin was transferred to the religious services of the Christians as though with the sanction of the Founder of the religion.

The ring dance was regarded as a sinister ceremony by the priestly authorities who were engaged in suppressing the Old Religion during the Middle Ages. Boguet compares the round dance of the witches with that of the fairies, whom he stigmatizes as 'devils incarnate'.[70] The ring usually moved to the left, but where, as in France, the dancers faced outwards the movement was *widdershins*, against the sun. The Aberdeen witches[71] were accused of dancing devilish dances round the Market and Fish Crosses of the town, and also round a great stone at Craigleauch.

The ring dance has shared the fate of many religious rites and has become an amusement for children. Some such dances have a person as the central object, round whom the whole ring turns. Those which have no central figure are usually imitative dances, like Mulberry Bush, where the original actions were undoubtedly not so simple and innocent as those now performed. In parts of Belgium the children still dance in a ring with the performers facing outwards.

The immense importance of the dance as a religious ceremony and an act of adoration of the Deity is seen by the attitude of the Church towards it. In 589 the third Council of Toledo[72] forbade the people to dance in churches on the vigils of saints' days. In 1209[73] the Council of Avignon promulgated a similar prohibition. As late as the seventeenth century the apprentices of York danced in the nave of the Minster.[74] Even at the present day the priest and choristers of the cathedral at Seville dance in front of the altar on Shrove Tuesday and at the feasts of Corpus Christi and of the Immaculate Conception; while at Echternach in Luxembourg on [75] Whit-Tuesday the priest, accompanied by choir and congregation, dances to church and round the altar.

The sacred dance is undoubtedly pre-Christian, and nothing can emphasize more strongly its hold on the minds of the people than its survival after many centuries of Christianity. Not only has it survived but it has actually been incorporated into the rites of the new religion, and we see it still danced by priests and worshippers of the new faith in their holiest precincts just as it was danced by priests and worshippers in the very earliest dawn of religion.

The music to which the worshippers danced was a source of great interest to some of the recorders, and accounts are

12. THE WITCH AND HER FAMILIAR

In the Crypt, York Minster

13. THE PRIZE BESOM OF SHAFTESBURY

very varied. It was not uncommon for the Grandmaster himself to be the performer, even when he led the dance; but there was often a musician who played for the whole company. The usual instruments were the flute, the pipe, the *trump* or Jew's harp, and in France the violin. But there were others in vogue also. The musical bow of the little masked figure of the Palaeolithic era (Plate 3) is very primitive, the player is dancing to his own music as the Devil so often did in Scotland. The flute as an instrument for magical purposes occurs in Egypt at the very dawn of history, when a masked man plays on it in the midst of animals. The pan-pipes, as their name implies, belong specially to a god who was disguised as an animal.

In Lorraine in 1589[76] the musical instruments were extraordinarily primitive. Besides small pipes, which were played by women, a man 'has a horse's skull which he plays as a cyther. Another has a cudgel with which he strikes an oaktree, which gives out a note and an echo like a kettle drum or a military drum. The Devil sings in a hoarse shout, exactly as if he trumpeted through his nose so that a roaring wooden voice resounds through the wide air. The whole troop together shout, roar, bellow, howl, as if they were demented and mad.' The French witches were apparently appreciative of good music for they told de Lancre[77] that 'they dance to the sound of the tambourine and the flute, and sometimes with a long instrument which they place on the neck and pulling it out down to the belt they strike it with a little stick; sometimes with a violin. But these are not the only instruments at the Sabbath, for we have learned from many that they hear there every kind of instrument, with such harmony that there is not a concert in the world that can equal it.'

The Feast. The feast was an important part of the religious ceremonies, and in this the cult of the Horned God was like other Pagan ceremonies of which records remain. The Mithraic Supper and the Christian Love-feasts were of the same class.

The Rites

Throughout all the ceremonies of this early religion there is an air of joyous gaiety and cheerful happiness which even the holy horror of the Christian recorders cannot completely disguise. When the witches' own words are given without distortion their feelings towards their religious rites and their god are diametrically opposed to the sentiments of the Christians. The joyousness of the cult is particularly marked in the descriptions of the feasts, perhaps because to the recorders there was nothing specially wicked in the ceremony, and they were at less pains to attribute infernal and devilish meanings to it than to other parts of the pagan ritual.

At the Great Sabbaths when whole villages met together for a combination of religion and amusement the feast must have been a source of great happiness, symbolizing as it did the gifts of God to man, with the god himself presiding in person. The acknowledgment to the Divine Man of his gifts is recorded in the evidence of Isobel Gowdie at Nairn; she stated that when they had finished eating, 'we looked steadfastly to the Devil, and bowing to him we said, "We thank thee, our lord, for this".'[78]

There seems to have been some doubt in the minds of the judges as to whether the feasts were not illusion on the part of the 'Foul Fiend', so that it is interesting to find that the inquisitor Boguet[79] reports, that 'very often at the Sabbath, they eat in good earnest, and not by fantasy and imagination.' The style of the feast varied according to the wealth of the giver. Boguet is again our informant when he says that the banquets were composed of various sorts of food, according to the place and rank of the participants, the table being covered with butter, cheese, and meat. Among the very poor there was often no feast, as in Alsace in 1618[80] when Catherine Volmar contracted a witch-marriage with the Devil Peterlin, 'there was no banquet because no one had brought food or drink.'

When weather permitted the food was eaten in the open air. The feasts of the witches of Wincanton, in Somerset,[81] sound very pleasant, 'all sate down, a white Cloth being spread on the ground, and did drink Wine, and eat Cakes and Meat.' In Scotland, where the weather was more uncertain, the records show that the feast usually took place indoors. The food was supplied by the Chief as a rule; sometimes one of the richer members of the coven would provide; and it was also not uncommon for the congregation to bring each his or her own food and eat it in company. In this last case the food was apt to be homely enough, as in Sweden,[82] where 'the diet they did use to have was, they said, Broth with Colworts and Bacon in it, Oatmeal, Bread spread with Butter, Milk, and Cheese.' When the Grandmaster provided the food the feast was worthy of the giver, and if a rich member was the hostess the food was always of the best. Thus Elspeth Bruce[83] gave her fellow-members a goose in her own house, and found great favour in the eyes of the Master, partly on account of her good dinner, but also because she was 'ane prettie woman'. The Lancashire witches[84] had a simple method of providing for their feast, they merely took what they required from some local farmer, 'the persons aforesaid had to their dinners beef, bacon, and roasted mutton; which mutton was of a wether of Christopher Swyers of Barley; which wether was brought in the night before into his mother's house by James Device, and killed and eaten.' In the same way the witches of Forfar[85] helped themselves to what they wanted, 'they went to Mary Rynd's house and sat down together at the table, the Devil being present at the head of it; and some of them went to John Benny's house, he being a brewer, and brought ale from thence, and others of them went to Alexander's Hieche's and brought *aqua vitae* from thence, and thus made themselves merry.'

The Somerset witches in 1664[86] were always the guests of their chief, who treated them well, 'at their meeting they have usually Wine or good Beer, Cakes, Meat or the like. They eat and drink really when they meet in their bodies, dance also and have Musick.' Another account says that 'they had Wine, Cakes, and Roastmeat (all brought by the

Man in Black) which they did eat and drink. They danced
and were merry, and were bodily there and in their Clothes.'
Even as early as 1588[87] Alison Peirson, who went among the
fairies, said that a man in green 'appeared to her, a lusty
man, with many men and women with him; she blessed herself and prayed, and passed with them further than she could
tell; and saw with them piping and merriness and good cheer,
and was carried to Lothian, and saw wine puncheons with
tasses with them.' Marie Lamont[88] in 1662 said that 'the
Devil came to Kattrein Scott's house in the midst of the
night, he was in the likeness of a mickle black man, and sung
to them and they danced. He gave them wine to drink and
wheat bread to eat, and they were all very merry.' At
Borrowstowness in 1679[89] there was a large party, the accusation was that 'ye and each person of you was at several
meetings with the Devil in the links of Borrowstowness, and
in the house of you, Bessie Vickar, and ye did eat and drink
with the Devil, and with one another, and with witches in
her house in the night time; and the Devil and William Craw
brought the ale which ye drank, extending to seven gallons.'
Very different was the picnic feast of the Andover coven in
New England;[90] Goody Foster, of Salem, was asked what
she did for victuals at the meeting, 'she answered that she
carried Bread and Cheese in her pocket, and that she and
the Andover Company came to the Village before the Meeting began, and sat down together under a tree and eat their
food, and that she drank water out of a Brook to quench her
thirst. And that the Meeting was upon a plain grassy place,
by which was a Cart path and sandy ground in the path, in
which were the tracks of Horses' feet. And she also told me
how long they were going and returning.'

The general belief among the Christian recorders was that
at a witch-feast salt was not permitted, and various reasons
were adduced to account for the omission. The sanctity of
salt was a pre-Christian idea, and the taboo on its use was
strictly observed by the Egyptian priests. Salt has a special
significance among Moslems and other non-Christian

peoples, and the belief in its holiness has continued into Christian times and even to the present day, for it is used in the making of the baptismal chrism. The spilling of salt is still considered unlucky, and the sowing of salt on the site of a sacked town probably meant that the place was taboo and might not be cultivated. The accounts of the witch-feasts show that salt was commonly used, though here and there it appears to have been omitted. Sometimes a reason for its absence is given, as in the case of the Alsatian witch, Anna Lang, in 1618,[91] who had no bread or salt at the feast in the woods of Saint-Hippolite, because things had fallen out of the cart on the way there.

Wine was ordinarily drunk at feasts, especially when the provisions were given by the rich members of the flock. In France it was usually drunk out of wooden goblets, but in Alsace[92] the wealthy ladies brought with them their own silver cups, out of which everybody drank. In England and Scotland beer or *aqua vitae* were the usual drinks.

The combination of religion and feasting and general jollity so characteristic of the Great Sabbaths is curiously reminiscent of the modern method of keeping Christmas.

V

Religious and Magical Ceremonies

Blessed be the Christians and all their ways and works,
Cursed be the Infidels, Hereticks, and Turks.

KIPLING (slightly altered)

It has so far been impossible for anyone to devise a theory
which will decide where Magic ends and Religion begins.
The best explanation is that Magic acts as a natural
means, that the mere pronouncing of a spell or the performance of certain movements will produce the desired effect as
surely as the mixture of two chemical substances will produce
a definitely ascertained result. Magic therefore acts alone,
it engenders its own force and depends on nothing outside
itself, whereas Religion acknowledges a Power beyond itself
and acts entirely by the motivation of that Power. The form
in which the Power presents itself to the human mind depends on the state of civilization to which the worshipper
has attained. Man at some periods and in some places
believes that the Power may be forced to obey his behests,
that it cannot resist the commands of the man who performs
certain ceremonies accompanied by certain words and
manual gestures. At other periods and other places Man
regards the Power as greater than himself and tries to pro-
pitiate it by means of prayers and gifts, which may include
sacrifices of all kinds and self-abasement in every form.

The theory is accurate up to a point, but does not account
for all the phenomena. I have therefore not attempted to
divide the ceremonies of the witches in accordance with it,
but have adopted the conventional division of calling those
ceremonies 'religious' which were done more or less as acts
of worship, and those 'magical' which were for the control

of the forces of nature, such as producing storms, or for casting on or curing disease.

Religious Ceremonies. The religious rites, which we should call divine service at the present day, were solemnized with the greatest reverence. Homage to the Master was always paid at the beginning of all the sacred functions, and this often included the offering of a burning candle. At Poictiers in 1574[1] the Devil was in the form of 'a large black goat who spoke like a person', and to whom the witches rendered homage holding a lighted candle. Boguet says in 1598[2] that the witches worshipped a goat, 'and for greater homage they offer to him candles which give a flame of a blue colour. Sometimes he holds a black image which he makes the witches kiss, and when kissing it they offer a candle or a wisp of burning straw.' The Somerset witches in 1664[3] said that when they met the Man in Black at the Sabbath 'they all make low obeysance to him, and he delivers some Wax Candles like little Torches, which they give back again at parting.' As a rule the candles were lighted at a fire or light which the Grandmaster carried on his head between his horns; which shows that the rite was reserved for the great Sabbaths when the Devil was 'in his grand Array'. De Lancre (*Tableau*, p. 68) says that the Devil usually had three horns, with 'a kind of light on the middle one, by which he is accustomed to illuminate the Sabbath and to give fire and light to those witches who hold lighted candles at the ceremonies of the mass which they counterfeit.' Usually the Devil lit the candles himself and handed them to his worshippers, but sometimes the witches were permitted to light their own candles. In either case the symbolism conveyed the meaning that to his worshippers their god was the source of all light.

During the ceremony of receiving homage the god was enthroned. After the ceremony of the candles the congregation knelt before his throne chanting his praises. Then there were hymns and prayers, and sometimes the Master gave an address on the tenets and dogmas of the religion. This was more common in Scotland than elsewhere, as sermons have always been popular in that country, but preachers were known in France also. The style and subject matter of some of these sermons have been preserved. De Lancre[4] says the subject was usually vainglory, but the Scotch records are more detailed. In the trial of John Fian, of the North Berwick coven, in 1590,[5] it was stated that 'Satan stood as in a pulpit making a sermon of doubtsome speeches, saying, "Many comes to the fair, but buys not all wares", and desired him "not to fear though he was grim; for he had many servants who should never want and should ail nothing, and he should never let any tear fall from their eyes as long as they served him." And gave their lessons and commandments to them as follows, "Spare not to eat, drink, and be blyth, taking rest and ease, for he should raise them up at the latter day gloriously".' In the trial of some Lothian witches[6] the preacher is said to have preached 'the doctrines of the infernall Pitt, viz., Blasphemies against God and his son Christ', in other words, he held forth on what he considered to be the true faith and abused the other side. 'Among other things he told them that they were more happy in him than they could be in God; him they saw, but God they could not see.' In another sermon by the same preacher,[7] he 'most blasphemously mocked them, if they offered to trust in God who left them miserable in the world, and neither he nor his Son Jesus Christ ever appeared to them when they called on them, as he had, who would not cheat them.' This was undoubtedly the great appeal of the Old Religion; the god was there present with his worshippers, they could see him, they could speak to him as friend to friend, whereas the Christian God was unseen and far away in Heaven, and the petitioner could never be sure that his prayer would reach the divine ear.

The main part of the religious rite was a ceremony comparable with the Mass. It must, however, be noted that this rite was not in any way an attempt to represent the Last Supper as described in the Gospels, except that it included the distribution of bread and wine; therefore Cotton Mather is wrong when he says that they 'imitated the Supper of our Lord'. The most detailed accounts of the ceremony come from more than one place in France.[8] Everything was black; the bread was black, being made of rye; the drink was black and pungent, being probably some kind of drink like the holy heather-beer of the Picts; the lights were black, for they were torches dipped in resin or pitch which gives a blue flame. The Chief was disguised as a black goat[9] and displayed the sacred bread on his horns; he took the sacred wine and sprinkled it on the kneeling people, while they cried out in chorus, 'His blood be on us and on our children.' Throughout the ceremony the people knelt bowing their heads to the ground, or they lay prostrate, all uniting in a prayer to their god for aid. The descriptions show that the congregations were endued with a passionate devotion to their deity and their religion, and one can see that the Inquisitor de Lancre[10] was not exaggerating when he summarizes the feelings of the witches who suffered for their faith. 'In short,' he says, 'it is a false martyrdom; and there are witches so besotted in his devilish service that neither torture nor anguish affright them, and who say that they go to a true martyrdom and death for love of him as gaily as to a festival of pleasure and public rejoicing. When they are seized by Justice they neither weep nor shed a single tear, in truth their martyrdom, whether by torture or the gibbet, is so joyful to them that many of them long to be led to execution, and suffer very joyously when they are brought to trial, so much do they long to be with the Devil. And in prison they are impatient of nothing so much as that they may show how much they suffer and desire to suffer for him.' This is the spirit which is held up to admiration when it inspires the Christian martyr, but when it was a heathen woman dying for her god she is execrated as the worshipper of the Devil and is thought to have deserved the most cruel of all deaths for her contumacy in not accepting a God of whom she knew nothing.

Sacrifices. There were several different forms of sacrifice, all of which involved the shedding of blood. The simplest, which was done with hardly any religious ceremony, was the pricking of her own person by the worshipper. This might be done either in private or in public. The sacrifice of animals was also a private rite, and never took place at a Great Sabbath, though it is occasionally recorded at an Esbat. The sacrificial animals were usually a dog, a cat, or a fowl. The animal was offered but not necessarily killed; in the account of the storm-raising by the witches of North Berwick the cat, which had been specially prepared by various magical ceremonies, was cast into the sea as far as possible, but it simply swam back and came safely to land.

Child sacrifice was not uncommon if the accusations are to be credited, but little real evidence is brought forward of the actual killing of children, and it must always be remembered that child-sacrifice is an accusation which the members of a dominant religion are very apt to bring against any other religion with which they are at variance. Occasionally, however, it would seem that a very young infant might be put to death as a religious rite; but this was very rare, and is not recorded in England. It occurs in one trial in Scotland in 1658,[11] when the Alloa coven were accused that 'they all together had a meeting at Tullibodie, where they killed a child, another at Clackmannan, where they killed another child.' Many accusations against the witches included the charge of eating the flesh of infants. This does not seem to have been altogether unfounded, though there is no proof that children were killed for the purpose. Similar forms of cannibalism as a religious rite were practised by the worshippers of Bacchus in ancient Greece.

There is one form of cannibalism which seems to have arisen after the persecutions had begun. Some of the witches deliberately ate the flesh of a young infant with the avowed purpose of obtaining the gift of silence, even under torture, when questioned by the Christian judges. The child does not appear to have been killed for the purpose, but considering the infant mortality of the period there could have been no difficulty in obtaining the magical flesh. The reason for the practice was a form of sympathetic magic, by eating the flesh of a child who had never spoken articulate words the witches' own tongues would be prevented also from articulating. De Lancre[12] shows this belief very clearly, 'In order not to confess the secrets of the school, they make at the Sabbath a paste of black millet with the powder made from the dried liver of an unbaptized child; it has the virtue of taciturnity; so that whosoever eats it will never confess.' This generalization is borne out by the evidence at two Scotch trials. At Forfar in 1661[13] Helen Guthrie stated that she and some others dug up the body of an unbaptized infant, 'and took several parts thereof, as the feet, hands, a part of the head, and a part of the buttock, and they made a pie thereof, that they might eat of it, that by this means they might never make confession (as they thought) of their witchcrafts.' In 1695 one of the Bargarran witches[14] told the court that 'their Lord (as they called him) gave them a piece of an unchristened Child's liver to eat; telling them, That though they were Apprehended, they should never Confess, which would prevent an effectual Discovery.'

The greatest of all the sacrifices was that of the god himself. This took place at one of the great quarterly Sabbaths at the end of a term of years, generally seven or nine. Frazer has shown that the Dying God was originally the ruler of the tribe, in other words the king. When the custom begins to die out in any country, the first change is the substitution of some person of high rank who suffers in the king's stead; for a few days before his death the substitute enjoys royal powers and honours as he is for the time being actually the king. The next step is when a volunteer, tempted by the desire for royal power though only temporary, takes the king's fate upon himself. Then comes the substitution of a criminal already condemned to die in any case, and the final stage is the sacrifice of an animal.

When the records of the Old Religion were made the great sacrifice had reached the last stages. In France a goat was burnt to death at the Sabbaths, the creature being called the Devil. The ashes were collected for the magical promotion of fertility by strewing them on fields and animals. The gathering up of the ashes in the case of Joan of Arc should be remembered in this connection. It is perhaps worth remarking that when, in the seventeenth century, the time for the sacrifice had come the god is always said to be in the form of a large goat or in his 'grand array', which means that in the original rite it was the sacrifice of the Horned God himself.

In the primitive forms of the sacrifice elsewhere than in Europe the worshippers ate the dead body of the god, or at least some part of it. Ceremonial cannibalism is found in many parts of the world, and in all cases it is due to the desire to obtain the qualities of the dead person, his courage, his wisdom, and so on. When a divine victim was eaten and the holy flesh thus received into the system, the worshipper became one with the deity. In ancient Egypt, as in other places, it was more common to eat the animal substitute or a figure of the god made in dough or other edible substance. The sacrifice of the god in the person of the king or his substitute was known from very early times, and has continued in some countries until the present century. It remained in western Europe as long as the cult of the Horned God lasted, and I have collected in the chapter on the Divine Victim several examples of the royal gods and their divine substitutes. Besides these historical instances there must have been many local victims who, being in a humble walk of life, were not recorded.

In modern books on this subject the substitutes are often called Mock Kings, whose rule was usually a kind of Saturnalia, for the royal powers were largely burlesqued. Klunzinger [15] records examples of the kind in Egypt in 1878, he says that in every village of Upper Egypt a New-Year King was elected, who for three or four days usurped the power of the Government and ruled despotically. He wore a special dress, and was treated with extravagant respect, he tried legal cases and passed ridiculous sentences on the offenders. At the end of his term of power he was tried and condemned to be burnt. He was then escorted by the whole village to the burning place and a ring of fire was made round him. When the flames became uncomfortably hot he jumped through them to safety, leaving his burlesque royal insignia to be destroyed. This is a very late form of the sacrifice; but in pre-Christian Europe the incarnate god was undoubtedly burnt alive, and it is very certain that the custom did not die out with the coming of Christianity. The burnt sacrifice performed by the 'Druids' was, I suggest, the offering of the substitutes for the Divine King.

The 'lease of life' granted to certain witches appears to have been another form of substitution for the royal or divine victim. In the evidence at some of the trials the Devil is said to have promised that for a term of years the witch should have wealth and power, but at the end of the time he should claim her, body and soul. Tradition says that he came in person to 'fetch' her, and there are many gruesome stories of his coming at the appointed hour. A usual feature of the story is that marks of burning were found afterwards on the dead body of the witch or that nothing was left of her but a heap of ashes. In many instances where the exact length of the lease of life is mentioned, the term is for seven years or multiples of seven. This coincides with the fact that in the case of the royal gods in England there seems to have been a seven-year cycle.

The sacrifice *of* the god was liable to be confused with a sacrifice *to* the god by those who were not fully acquainted with the cult. The recorders claimed that all child-murders, of which the witches were accused, were sacrifices to the devil. Child-murders were, however, seldom substantiated and were not more frequent among the witches than among other classes of society. When the actual testimony of the witches is given, and not the generalizations of biased Christians, there is no doubt that the person or animal who died was regarded as the god.

In traditional accounts of the fairies the seven-year cycle and the human sacrifice to the god are preserved. Thomas of Ercildoune[16] was carried away by the Fairy Queen; he remained with her for more than three years, she then sent him back to his own home, and when he remonstrated she told him that the next day was Hallow e'en:

> To-morrow, of hell the foulé fiend
> Among these folks shall choose his fee.
> Thou art a fair man and a hende,*
> I trow full well he would choose thee.

And in the ballad of *Young Tamlane*[17] the hero is a fairy knight who loves a human lady and asks her to save him:

> Then would I never tire, Janet,
> In elvish land to dwell;
> But aye at every seven years
> They pay the teind† to hell,
> And I am sae fat and fu' o' flesh
> I fear 'twill be mysell.

In view of the fact that ceremonial cannibalism was practised, Young Tamlane's physical condition has a sinister significance.

In a Cumberland tale[18] it is said that 'every seven years the elves and fairies pay Kane,‡ or make an offering of one of their children to the grand enemy of salvation, and they are permitted to purloin one of the children of men to present to the fiend; a more acceptable offering, I'll warrant, than one of their own infernal brood that are Satan's sib-allies, and drink a drop of the deil's blood every May morning.'

In early times the Dying God or his substitute was burnt alive in the presence of the whole congregation; but when western Europe became more organized such a ceremony could not be permitted and the victim died at the hands of the public executioner. The custom of burning the witch was not the invention of the Church, which only took advan-

---

* Hende = comely. † Teind = Tenth, tithe. ‡ Kane = Tax.

tage of a custom already existing and did nothing to modify the cruelty of more barbarous times. Death by burning was considered by the witches themselves as so essential that Ann Foster, of Northampton,[19] when condemned to die for witchcraft in 1674, 'mightily desired to be burned, but the Court would give no Ear to that, but that she should be hanged at the Common place of Execution.' This is in accordance with the request of a witch in the Rudlieb,[20] who when about to be hanged asked that her body should be taken down from the gallows and burnt, and the ashes strewn on water, lest being scattered in the air they should breed clouds, drought and hail.

It is interesting to note that there is no legal record that a witch was condemned to be burnt alive in England; witches were hanged if another crime besides witchcraft could be proved against them. In fact, the English leniency towards the 'horrible crime of witchcraft' is very noticeable. It was commented on in Scotland during the rule of the Commonwealth,[21] 'there is much witchery up and down our land; the English be too sparing to try it.' In Scotland persons could be condemned for witchcraft only, the usual method of execution was strangulation at the stake, after which the body was burnt; but there are cases on record where the witch was condemned to be burnt alive, and the records also show that the sentence was faithfully carried out. In France also evidence of the practice of witchcraft meant sentence of death, and the condemned person died in the flames. There is even a record of a man-witch who was sentenced '*à estre bruslé vif à petit feu*', and in Alsace[22] one of the magistrates said that burning was too good for witches, and condemned them to be torn in pieces with red-hot pincers. This is, as far as I know, the only occasion when the Christian clergy pleaded for mercy for the culprits; they were so far successful that the sentence was mitigated to beheading with the sword, for which mercy the condemned thanked the magistrate with tears of gratitude.

The belief in the dogma of the **Dying God** is the reason

why it is so often recorded against witches as a heinous sin that they pretended to be Christian while all the time they were 'Devil-worshippers'. The fundamental difference between the two religions is that the Christian believes that God died once for all, whereas the more primitive belief is that the god is perpetually incarnate on earth and may therefore be put to death over and over again. In all probability these 'Devil-worshippers' were quite honest in belonging to both religions, not realizing any difference in one of the basic doctrines of the new faith.

The Orgies.[23] The orgiastic ceremonies excited the interest and curiosity of the Christian judges and recorders to an extent out of all proportion to their importance in the cult. It is certain that in the religion of the Horned God, as in the cults of Bacchus and other deities of fertility, rites were performed which to the modern mind are too gross to be regarded as religious. These rites were openly practised in Athens in the height of its civilization, the Sacred Marriage being regarded as the means of promoting and increasing fertility. Similar rites are known and have been practised in all parts of the world, but always in what are now called 'Religions of the Lower Culture'. As the cult of the Horned God was also a religion of the Lower Culture such rites formed an integral part of the worship. The reason for their use is the same wherever found; it is the practical application of the theory of sympathetic magic, with the consequent belief that by such means the fertility of the whole land would be increased. It was on account of these rites that the witches were credited with—and claimed—the power of granting fertility. They had therefore also the opposite power, that of blasting fertility; for, as I have pointed out before, the primitive mind ascribed both good and evil to one power alone; the division into God and Devil, priest and witch, belongs to a higher stage of civilization.

Joan of Arc was definitely accused of having practised these rites, and it was through the agency of the Duchess of Bedford that her accusers were proved wrong. The accusa-

tion on this subject against Gilles de Rais was obviously
trumped up and had therefore to be combined with charges
of murder to force a conviction.

In all the trials where these rites are mentioned the Inquisitors of the Roman Church and the ministers of the
Reformed Church express an extreme of sanctimonious horror, coupled, however, with a surprisingly prurient desire to
learn all the most intimate details. The ceremonies may have
been obscene, but they are rendered infinitely worse by the
attitude of the ecclesiastical recorders and judges.

Magic Ceremonies. In the trials of witches the magical
element plays a large part. In all studies of witches and
magic, one point must be kept in mind, that when anything
regarded as out of the ordinary course of nature is brought
about by human means it is called a miracle if the magician
belongs to the beholder's own religion, but it is magic—
often black magic—if the wizard belongs to another religion.
In Grimm's words, 'Miracle is divine, Magic is devilish.'
This is markedly the case in the Christian records of the
wonders performed by witches.

The cauldron is one of the most important accessories of
a witch in popular estimation, but in spite of its prominence
in *Macbeth* it does not often appear in the trials. In Alsace,[24]
at the end of the sixteenth century it was greatly in vogue,
and its use is clearly explained. The ingredients used are not
given; the pot was boiled in the presence of all the company,
including the Devil, to the accompaniment of prayers and
charms. When ready, the cauldron was either overturned and
the contents spilt on the ground, or the liquid was distributed
to the votaries for sprinkling where they desired. The spilling was to bring fog, the rising steam being the sympathetic
magic to bring it about. The making of the liquid for sprinkling was obviously a religious ceremony, and when the cult
was in its prime and the witches were the priesthood the
sacred liquid was used for blessing the crops as holy water
is now. As with so many of the witch-ceremonies the original
meaning was lost, the new religion adopted the old rites with

slight changes and the older form of the ceremonial fell into disrepute and was sternly forbidden by the Church. The cauldron was not for magical rites only, it also served the homely purpose of cooking the food at the Sabbaths. 'There was a great cauldron on the fire to which everyone went and took out meat,' said the French witches to Boguet.[25] Nothing suggests more strongly the primitiveness of the rites and of the people who practised them than the use of the cooking-pot which was in common to the whole company (Plate 6*b*). The importance of cauldrons in the Late Bronze Age and Early Iron Age should be noted in this connection.

In all the activities of a farm which were directly connected with fertility, witches seem to have been called in to perform the rites which would secure the success of the operation. They were also consulted if an animal fell sick. Thus at Burton-on-Trent, in 1597,[26] a certain farmer's cow was ill, 'Elizabeth Wright took upon her to help upon condition that she might have a penny to bestow upon her god, and so she came to the man's house, kneeled down before the cow, crossed her with a stick in the forehead and prayed to her god, since which time the cow continued well.' Here there is the interesting and very definite statement that Elizabeth Wright had a god who was clearly not that of the Christians. In Orkney, in 1629,[27] Jonet Rendall was accused that 'the devil appeared to you, whom you called Walliman. . . . After you met your Walliman upon the hill you came to William Rendall's house, who had a sick horse, and promised to heal him if he could give you two pennies for every foot. And having gotten the silver you healed the horse by praying to your Walliman. And there is none that gives you alms but they will thrive, either by land or sea, if you pray to your Walliman.' Here again the god of the witch was not the same as that of the Christian.

The making of wax images for the destruction of an enemy has always been supposed to be a special art of a witch. The action has its origin in the belief in sympathetic magic; the image—of clay or wax—was made in the likeness of the doomed person, it was pierced with thorns or pins, and was finally dissolved in water or melted before a slow fire. The belief was that whatever was done to the image would be repeated in the body of the enemy, and as the image slowly melted he would get weaker and die. The method was probably quite effectual if the doomed man knew that magic, in which he believed, was being practised against him; but when the method was not successful the witches were often prepared to supplement magic with physical means, such as poison and cold steel.

Wax images for magical purposes are very early. There is reference to a wax crocodile in ancient Egypt as early as the XIIth dynasty (before 2000 B.C.), but the most detailed account is in the legal record of the Harem Conspiracy in the reign of the Pharaoh Rameses III (about 1100 B.C.). A plot was hatched to kill the Pharaoh and to put one of his sons on the throne; the conspirators were the young man's mother and several of the harem ladies and harem officials, besides people from outside. They began by making wax figures, but these not proving a success the conspirators resorted to personal violence, from the effects of which the Pharaoh eventually died. The conspirators were brought to justice, and the guilty were condemned to death. It is interesting to see how much less superstitious the ancient Egyptians were than the medieval Christians. There is no mention of the Devil, no feeling that an evil power was invoked; there is none of that shuddering horror which is so marked a feature of the Christian records, and the only abusive term used is the word 'criminal' applied to the convicted prisoners. There were two men concerned in the making of the wax figures. The record of the first one states[28] that 'he began to make magic rolls for hindering and terrifying, and to make some gods of wax and some people, for enfeebling the limbs of people; and gave them into the hand of Pebekkamen and the other great criminals, saying, "Take them in", and they took them in. Now, when he set himself to do the evil deeds which he did, in which Rê did not permit that he should succeed, he was examined. Truth was found in every crime and in every evil deed, which his heart had devised to do. There was truth therein, he had done them all, together with all the other great criminals. They were great crimes of death, the things which he had done. Now, when he learned of the great crimes of death which he had committed, he took his own life.' The other man was equally guilty, 'Now, when Penhuibin said to him, "Give me a roll for enduing me with strength and might", he gave to him a magic roll of the Pharaoh (Rameses III), and he began to employ the magic powers of a god upon people. He began to make people of wax, inscribed, in order that they might be taken by the inspector, hindering one troop and bewitching the others. Now, when he was examined, truth was found in every crime and every evil deed, which his heart had devised to do. There was truth therein, he had done them all, together with the other great criminals. The great punishments of death were executed upon him.'

In Great Britain the making of a wax figure was never done by one person alone, several members of the coven were present and everything was performed with great ceremony under the personal superintendence of the Grandmaster. The earliest example is of King Duffus of Scotland (961–5).[29] The king had fallen ill of a mysterious sickness; and a girl having let fall some suspicious words, 'some of the Guard being sent, found the Lass's Mother with some Hags, such as herself, roasting before a small moderate Fire, the King's picture made of Wax. The design of this horrid Act was that as the Wax by little and little did melt away, so the King's Body by a continual sweating might at last totally decay. The Waxen-Image being found and broken, and these old Hags being punished by death, the King did in that moment recover.' At North Berwick[30] Agnes Sampson was accused with others of being present at the making of an image. 'Anny Sampson affirmed that she, in company with nine other witches, being convened in the night beside Prestonpans, the Devil their master being present, standing in the midst of them; there a body of wax, shaped and made by the said Anny Sampson, wrapped within a linen cloth, was first delivered to the devil; which, after he had pronounced his verde, delivered the said picture to Anny Sampson, and she to her next marrow, and so everyone round about, saying, "This is King James the Sixth, ordered to be consumed at the instance of a nobleman, Francis, Earl Bothwell".' The image according to Barbara Napier's evidence [31] was 'devised for roasting and undoing of his Highness' person.' John Stewart at Irvine in 1618[32] said that when the witches were making clay images 'the Devil appeared among them in the similitude and likeness of a black little whelp.' They cut a lock of Stewart's hair to mix with the clay, 'and took the remnant of his said hair and singed it at the fire, and thereafter cast the same to the said black little whelp.' The Somerset witches, in 1664,[33] confessed to making and using several such images. 'The Devil baptized a Picture by the name of Ann or Rachel Hatcher. This Picture one Dunsford's Wife brought, and stuck Thorns in it—When they would bewitch Man, Woman, or Child, they do it sometimes by a Picture made in Wax, which the Devil formally baptizeth.—Ann Bishop brought in her Apron a Picture in blackish Wax, which the Devil baptized by the Name of John Newman, and then the Devil first, after Ann Bishop, thrust Thorns into the Picture, Ann Bishop sticking in two Thorns into the Arms of it.—Margaret Agar brought thither an Image in Wax, and the Devil, in the shape of a Man in black Clothes, did baptize it, and after stuck a Thorn into its Head; that Agar stuck one into its Stomach, and Catherine Green one into its Side.—A Picture in Wax or Clay was delivered to the Man in black, who stuck a Thorn into the Crown of it, Agar one towards the Breast, Catherine Green in the side; after which Agar threw down the Picture, and said, *There is Cornish's Picture with a Murrain to it,* or a Plague on it.—Margaret Agar delivered to the little Man in black, a Picture in Wax, into which he and Agar stuck Thorns, and Henry Walter thrust his

Thumb into the side of it; then they threw it down, and said, *There is Dick Green's Picture with a Pox on it.*' In 1678[34] some members of the witch coven of Paisley met together to make an image for the destruction of Sir George Maxwell. A man-witch gave evidence 'that the Devil required every one of their consents for the making of the Effigies of Clay, for the taking away the Life of Sir George Maxwell. Declares, that every one of the Persons above-mentioned gave their Consents to the making of the said Effigies, and that they wrought the Clay, and that the black Man did make the figure of the Head and Face, and two Arms on the said Effigies. Declares, That the Devil set three Pins in the same, one in each Side, and one in the Breast; And that the Declarant did hold the Candle to them, all the time the Picture was making.' In New England in 1692,[35] the accusation against the Rev. George Burroughs included the charge 'that he brought Poppets to them, and Thorns to stick into those Poppets.' In medieval times it is very certain that the recorders regarded wax images as being made only for evil purposes, but it is possible that they were also used for healing the sick. It was a common thing for a witch to be accused of casting pain or illness from the patient on some other person or on an animal. When, as often happened, the pains were those of childbirth and were cast on the husband he was most indignant, and his indignation was shared by the male judges to whom he related his woes. That a man should be called upon to suffer 'the natural and kindly pains' which ought to be peculiarly the lot of women was too terrible to be allowed, and the witch who did this particular piece of magic was put to death. The case of the transference of cancer from one patient to another is mentioned on page 73. Unfortunately, though the accusations of transference of illness are fairly common, the method is never described in full. It may, however, have been by means of a wax image, as done at the present day in Egypt, where an image of the patient is made, pins are stuck into it in the places where the pain is acute, and then the figure is destroyed in the fire, in the belief that the pain or disease has been put into the figure and will be destroyed by its destruction. It seems, therefore, not unlikely that, like other magical ceremonies of the witches, the wax images had their good uses as well as bad.

A ceremony, which had clearly once been for promoting the fertility of a cornfield, was used at Auldearne,[36] but when recorded it had degenerated into a method for destruction. 'Before Candlemas we went be-east Kinloss, and there we yoked a plough of toads. The Devil held the plough, and John Young, our Officer, did drive the plough. Toads did draw the plough as oxen, couch-grass was the harness and trace-chains, a gelded animal's horn was the coulter, and a piece of a gelded animal's horn was the sock.' In this everything denoted sterility, but the method was clearly derived from a fertility rite.

Many of the magical charms and spells were for the healing of the sick or for the prevention of disease. Thus Barbara Paterson was accused in 1607[37] of getting water from the Dow-loch, and 'putting the said loch-water into a stoup, and causing the patients lift it up and say, "I lift this stoup in the name of the Father, Son and Holy Ghost, for the health of them for whom it was lifted", which words were to be repeated three times nine. Item, she used this charm for curing cattle, "I charm ye for arrow-shot, for eye-shot, for tongue-shot, for liver-shot, for lung-shot, for cat-shot, all the most, in the name of the Father, Son, and Holy Ghost".' Though this might very reasonably have been called a Christian prayer, it was reckoned as a devilish charm when used by a witch. Another charm[38] for the preservation of the reciter was used by Agnes Sampson, and was known as the White Paternoster; it is clearly a confused version of a Christian prayer or hymn:

> *White Paternoster,*
> *God was my Foster.*
> *He fostered me*
> *Under the Book of Palm-tree.*

Saint Michael was my Dame,
He was born at Bethelem.
He was made of flesh and blood.
God send me my right food;
My right food, and dyne two,
That I may to yon Kirk go
To read upon yon sweet Book,
*Which the mighty God of Heaven shoop.**
Open, open, Heaven's Yaits.
Steik,† steik, Hell's Yaits, ‡
All Saints be the better,
That hear the White Prayer, Pater Noster.

The companion-charm[38] is the Black Paternoster, which
has the distinction of surviving to the present day in various
forms as a charm to be said before going to sleep. This seems
to be the meaning of the epithets given to the two prayers,
the White Paternoster being the morning prayer to be said
in daylight, the Black Paternoster the prayer for the night-
time. The Black Paternoster is as follows:

Four neuks in this house for haly Angels,
A post in the midst, that's Christ Jesus,
Lucas, Marcus, Matthew, Joannes,
God be into this house, and all that belangs us.

Many charms and spells surviving to the present day con-
tain the names of pre-Christian gods. These spells are usually
connected with cures for diseases in human beings and
animals, and are generally accompanied with certain manual
gestures without which the charm is of little avail. One of
the most interesting brings in the names of Woden and Loki,
and as the hammer is of importance in the charm it is
possible that Thor also is indicated.[39] It is a cure for ague:
'Nail three old horse-shoes to the foot of the patient's bed,
with the hammer placed crosswise on them. Take the hammer
in the left hand and tap the shoes, saying:

* Shoop= Shaped.   † Steik= Shut.   ‡ Yaits= Gates.

136

Father, Son, and Holy Ghost,
Nail the Devil to the post;
Thrice I strike with holy crook,
One for God, one for Wod, and one for Lok.

The destructive acts of the witches were often real, but
were supposed to be effected by magic. The means were very
simple, as in the cases following. At Crook of Devon in
Kinross-shire in 1661[40] Bessie Henderson 'confessed and
declared that Janet Paton was with you at a meeting when
they tramped down Thos. White's rye in the beginning of
the harvest, 1661, and that she had broad soles and tramped
down more nor any.' In the same year in Forfar[41] the coven
assisted the Devil to destroy a wooden bridge during a storm;
it was apparently done to strike terror into the people of the
neighbourhood. The method of effecting the destruction of
the bridge was simplicity itself; Helen Guthrie said that 'they
went to the bridge of Cortaquhie with intention to pull it
down, and that for this end she herself, Jonet Stout, and
others of them did thrust their shoulders against the bridge,
and that the Devil was busy among them acting his part.'
Isobel Smyth corroborated Helen Guthrie's account and
added, 'We all rued that meeting for we hurt ourselves lift-
ing.' Helen Guthrie also stated that 'the last summer except
one, she did see John Tailyour, sometimes in the shape of a
tod and sometimes in the shape of a swine, and the said John
Tailyour in these shapes went up and down among William
Milne, miller at Heatherstakes, his corn for the destruction
of the same; and the Devil came to her, and pointed out
John Tailyour in the foresaid shapes, and told her that that
was John Tailyour.' In 1692 at Hartford, Connecticut,[42]
Hugh Crosia (Crawshay) was accused of dealings with the
Devil, 'he also said the Devil opened the door of Eben
Booth's house, made it fly open and the gate fly open; being
asked how he could tell, he said the Devil appeared to him
like a boy, and told him he did make them fly open, and
then the boy went out of sight.' There were also a certain

number of charms and spells for acquiring benefits at one's neighbour's cost, and of this James Og of Aberdeen was accused in 1597.[43] 'Is indited to have passed on Rood-day through Alexander Cobaine's corn, and have taken nine stones from his own rig and cast on the said Alexander's rig, and to have taken nine locks (handfuls) of mould from the said Alexander's rig and cast it on his own. Is indicted to have passed on Lammas-day through the said Alexander's corn, and having gone nine space (paces ?), meting with a white wand, to have stricken the same nine times, so that nothing grew that year but fichakes.'

That the witches claimed to be, and were recognized as, rainmakers, is abundantly proved by the evidence given at the trials. Their methods varied considerably. According to Wierus,[44] the witches were said to bring rain 'by casting flint stones behind their backs towards the west, or flinging a little sand into the air, or striking a river with a broom and so sprinkling the wet of it towards heaven, stirring water with the finger in a hole in the ground, or boiling hogs' bristles in a pot.' Wierus was the great witch advocate, whose views on witches were far in advance of his time. Reginald Scot quotes largely from his works, and Scot's own book had the honour of being publicly burnt on account of the heretical views he promulgated as to witchcraft, in which he firmly disbelieved.

The rainmaker is also the storm-bringer, and the witches were always supposed to create storms when they wished. The magic was effected by a sacrifice and a prayer to the deity, which is exactly the same method by which the prophet Samuel produced a violent thunderstorm and discomfited the Philistines. It was a divine miracle when Samuel accomplished it, but it was a diabolical deed when the witches were the active agents. Had the Philistines recorded the event they would hardly have regarded Samuel as anything but a witch.

The North Berwick covens raised a great tempest to drown King James VI and his queen on their way to Scotland from Denmark. Agnes Sampson[45] confessed that 'at the time when his Majesty was in Denmark, she being accompanied by the parties before named, took a cat and christened it, and afterwards bound to each part of that cat the chiefest part of a dead man and several joints of his body: And in the night following, the said cat was conveyed into the midst of the sea by all the witches, and so left the said cat right before the town of Leith in Scotland. This done there did arise such a tempest in the sea, as a greater hath not been seen.' The legal record of a similar event is more detailed,[46] and mentions that the coven at Prestonpans sent a letter to the Leith coven that 'they should make the storm universal through the sea. And within eight days after the said Bill (letter) was delivered the said Agnes Sampson (and several others) baptised a cat in the webster's house, in manner following: First, two of them held a finger in the one side of the chimney crook, and another held another finger in the other side, the two nebs of the fingers meeting together; then they put the cat thrice through the links of the crook, and passed it thrice under the chimney. Thereafter, at Beigis Todd's house, they knit to the four feet of the cat four joints of men; which being done, Jonet Campbell fetched it to Leith; and about midnight, she and the two Linkops and the two wives called Stobbeis, came to the Pier-head, and saying these words, "See that there be no deceit among us"; and they cast the cat into the sea, so far as they might, which swam over and came again; and they that were in the Pans cast in another cat in the sea at XI hours. After which, by their sorcery and enchantment, the boat perished betwixt Leith and Kinghorn; which thing the Devil did, and went before with a staff in his hand.'

A form of magic, which is strictly localized and belongs only to England, was performed by means of a small animal. To this I have given the name of the *Domestic Familiar* to distinguish it from the Divining Familiar which is found universally throughout Europe (see p. 81).

Magic words did not play so large a part as might have been expected among the witches. This is perhaps due to

fear on the part of the recorders, who dared not repeat the
words lest they might have some undesired effect. There
seems no doubt that the name of the god was regarded as a
sure means of bringing him into the presence of the person
who called him, as in the case of Elizabeth Sawyer quoted
above on page 86. There were, however, other words used
to summon the god. Agnes Sampson[47] cried out, 'Elva, come
and speak to me', or, 'Hola, Master', when she wished him
to appear either in person or as her divining Familiar, and
dismissing him by telling him to 'depart by the law he lives
on'. Andro Man, at Aberdeen,[48] had two words, one to raise
the Devil, the other to dismiss him; the first, *Benedicite*, is
certainly Latin, but the second, *Maikpeblis*, is a corruption
of some misunderstood formula, probably Christian. Alexander Hamilton, of Lothian[49] was wont to strike thrice on
the ground with a baton of fir and to say, 'Rise up, foul
thief', when he called on his Master; and the dismissal took
the form of throwing a live cat in the direction of the divining
Familiar or of the Incarnate God. The Somerset witches[50]
called up their Familiars or even the Grandmaster himself
simply with the word *Robin*, and when he appeared they
added, 'O Satan, give me my purpose.'

Marie Lamont[51] called *Serpent*, when she summoned the
'Devil', and the Swedish witches[52] cried 'Antecessor, come
and carry us to Blockula.' Jean Weir[53] joined the confra-
ternity by putting her foot on a cloth in the presence of a
witness, and then uttering the words, 'All my cross and
troubles go alongst to the door.' A modern method[54] is to
walk three times round the church, and the third time to
stand still in front of the church door, and cry 'Come out',
or whistle through the keyhole.

The words used for flying varied in different parts of the
country, though in many cases the name of the God was invoked. The earliest record of the flying charm is in Guernsey
in 1563[55] when Martin Tulouff heard his mother say as she
mounted her broomstick, '*Va au nom du Diable et Lucifer
pardessus roches et Espynes.*' In 1586 the Alsace witch, Anna

Wickenzipfel,[56] flew on a white wand with two other women,
crying as they started, 'Thither, in the name of a thousand
Devils.' The Basque witches[57] had several formulae to be
used as occasion required, usually they said, *Emen hetan*,
Emen hetan, which de Lancre translates as, 'Here and there,
Here and there.' Those who were more devout called on
their god to whom they likened themselves, 'I am god (lit.:
the Devil), I have nothing which is not thine. In thy name,
O Lord, this thy servant annoints herself and some day will
be Devil and Evil Spirit like thee.' When crossing a stream
they said, '*Haute la coude, Quillet*', which prevented their
getting wet. Another magic phrase was for those who had
to go long distances (unfortunately de Lancre does not
translate it) 'Pic suber hoeilhe, en ta la lane de bouc bien
m'arrecoueille.' Isabel Gowdie of Auldearne in 1662[58] announced that she had two forms of words, one was 'Horse
and Hattock in the Devil's name'; the other was, 'Horse and
Hattock! Horse and go! Horse and Pellatis! Ho! Ho!' The
Somerset witches in 1664[59] had 'a long form of words' to
be used when starting but nothing is recorded but gibberish,
which suggests a misunderstood and mis-pronounced formula; it ran, 'Thout, tout a tout, tout, throughout and about.'
When leaving the meeting they said, 'A boy, merry meet,
merry part', and when they started homewards, they shouted
'*Rentum tormentum*', and another word which the witness had
forgotten.

There were other formulae to be used for healing or as
prayer. The words were generally taught by the Devil himself to his disciples, as in the case of Elizabeth Sawyer, the
witch of Edmonton, in 1621,[60] 'He, the Devil, taught me
this prayer, *Santibicetur nomen tuum*.' The Paternoster repeated in Latin was clearly regarded as a charm of great
power, for we find Mother Waterhouse[61] using it over her
Familiar, 'she said that when she would will him to do anything for her, she would say her Pater noster in Latin.' In
1597 the name of the God was sometimes changed and the
Christian Deity was invoked; Marion Grant,[62] who was

burnt for witchcraft, cured sick cattle in the name of the
Father, Son and Holy Ghost, and she also charmed a sword
by the same means. When crossing themselves the Basque
witches in 1609[63] repeated a prayer, which greatly shocked
the Inquisitor, who translates the words into French, '*Au
nom de Patrique Petrique d'Arragon, à cette heure, à cette heure,
Valence, tout notre mal est passé*', and '*Au nom de Patrique,
Petrique d'Arragon, Janicot de Castille faites-moi un baiser au
derrière.*' De Lancre records that a man-witch at Rion[64] 'confessed that he had cured many persons of fever by merely
saying these words *Consummatum est*, making the sign of the
Cross, and making the patient say three times *Pater noster*
and *Ave Maria.*' Another man-witch,[65] who was sentenced
to the galleys for life, said that he had such pity for the horses
which the postilions galloped along the road, that he did
something to prevent it, which was that he took vervain, and
said over it the *Paternoster* five times and the *Ave Maria* five
times, and then put it on the road, so that the horses should
cease to run. Isobel Gowdie of Auldearne in 1662[66] gave the
formula for transforming oneself into an animal. To become
a hare, the witch said:

> *I shall go into a hare,*
> *With sorrow and sighing and mickle care,*
> *And I shall go in the Divel's name,*
> *Aye, till I come home again.*

To revert to the human form, the witch repeated the words:

> *Hare, hare, God send thee care.*
> *I am in a hare's likeness just now,*
> *But I shall be in a woman's likeness even now.*

There were slight variations in the words if the witch wished
to be a cat or a crow. The method was simplicity itself, after
repeating the words the witch regarded herself as the animal
she had mentioned in the charm, but that there was no outward change is clear from the fact that if she met another

witch she had to say to her, 'I conjure thee, Go thou with me', otherwise the other witch would not have realized that she was an animal.

The Somerset witches in 1664[67] carried on the old tradition of making wax figures. The formula for naming a figure is given in some detail. The image was brought to the meeting, 'the Man in Black took it in his arms, anointed its forehead and said, "I baptize thee with this oil", and used some other words. He was Godfather, and this Examinant and Ann Bishop Godmothers.' The witches then proceeded to stick thorns into the image, saying as they did so, 'A pox on thee, I'll spite thee.' (See page 133.) The image to be effective had to be baptized with the name of the victim.

It must, however, be remembered that the witches were not peculiar in their belief that a form of words could affect the forces of Nature. Bede records[68] that on the occasion of a storm at sea, a Christian bishop 'showed himself the more resolute in proportion to the greatness of the danger, called upon Christ, and having in the name of the Holy Trinity, sprinkled a little water, quelled the raging waves.'

A modern version of a magical curse on an enemy is recorded by Lady Wilde[69] in Ireland, 'A woman went to the Saints' Well (in Innis-Sark), and, kneeling down, she took some of the water and poured it on the ground in the name of the devil, saying, "So may my enemy be poured out like water, and lie helpless on the earth." Then she went round the well backwards on her knees, and at each station she cast a stone in the name of the devil, and said, "So may the curse fall on him, and the power of the devil crush him".' Still more modern is the method of casting a curse by burning a candle in front of a saint's image in church; in the candle are stuck pins, and the enemy is supposed to waste away as the candle burns, exactly as was supposed to happen when a wax figure was melted with pins stuck in it.

There are many charms and spells still in vogue in which the name of the Christian Deity, usually the Trinity, is used, but in origin they belong to the pre-Christian religion.

Religious and Magical Ceremonies

Under a slight change of name much of the Old Religion still survives in Europe and can be found by any who are sufficiently interested to search for it. As an anthropological field of research Europe is almost untouched; yet in our midst the primitive cults still continue, though slightly overlaid by what we arrogantly term civilization. Africa may be the training ground for beginners, but the so-called 'advanced' countries offer to the investigator the richest harvest in the world.

14a. THE ELVES' DANCE
(Olaus Magnus, 1555)

14b. THE SACRILEGIOUS CAROLLERS

14c. THE HORN DANCE AT ABBOT'S
BROMLEY

15. MODERN LUCIA-QUEEN IN SWEDEN

With 'A Round of Waxen Tapers on her Head'

The Position of the Witch
in the Social Structure

The modern idea of the witch is founded entirely on the records of the seventeenth and eighteenth centuries, when the Christian Church was still engaged in crushing out the remains of Paganism and was reinforced in this action by the medical profession, who recognized in the witches their most dangerous rivals in the economic field. Throughout the country the witch or wise-woman, the *sage-femme*, was always called in at child-birth; many of these women were highly skilled, and it is on record that some could perform the Caesarian operation with complete success for both mother and child. But they also had the reputation of being able to relieve the 'natural and kindly pains of travail', by casting those pains on an animal, or still worse on the patient's husband; no wonder that every man's hand was against them. For this dreadful and impious act was against the Will of God, who in the beginning had cursed Eve and all her female descendants. Religion and medical science united against the witches, and when the law could no longer be enforced against them, they were vilified in every way that human tongue or pen could invent.

But for centuries both before and after the Christian era, the witch was both honoured and loved. Whether man or woman, the witch was consulted by all, for relief in sickness, for counsel in trouble, or for foreknowledge of coming events. They were at home in the courts of kings, where they sat on royal councils and gave advice on important matters of state, or they were among the serfs and peasants to whom they brought comfort and spiritual help. In primitive times, when there was no organization for dealing with misdemeanours and crime, their mystical power gave them the authority for discovering the culprits, who then received the appropriate punishment.

In dealing with the ancient and medieval religion, whether Pagan or Christian, the background of the life of the people must be remembered. Many of the phenomena, now known to be natural and governed by natural laws, were then regarded as supernatural and under the control of certain persons, who were variously known, as witches, magicians, astrologers, or prophets. The belief in divination, dreams, omens, charms, spells, curses, ghosts, evil spirits, and so forth, was part of the daily life of all classes of the community from the king down to the lowest and most abject of his subjects.

Divination was the peculiar right of the priesthood, for, as the word implies, it was the means of ascertaining the Will of God as regards future events. It was therefore essentially a religious rite, only to be performed by those in close touch with the Deity. In practice it seems that women-witches were most frequently consulted on personal matters, men-witches on affairs of political importance.

In ancient Egypt every temple had its prophets, its diviners, its interpreters of dreams, who were so numerous that they are usually recorded only on special occasions. One of the earliest prophets of high rank was the king's son, Ra-hotep, Great Seer, or High-priest of Heliopolis. Numerous references to magicians, diviners and prophets are found in that storehouse of ancient beliefs and customs, the Old Testament. One of the earliest was Joseph,[1] who, though not a priest, was in close touch with his God. He was not only an interpreter of dreams but also a diviner, using the Egyptian method of a silver bowl. Moses was a peculiarly potent magician, and like the Egyptian magicians, he performed his more outstanding wonder-working by means of his wand.[2] The wand then as now was the implement by which the power of the witch, fairy, or magician, was conveyed. The rod, or wand, of Moses has so many legends attached to it that it was obviously regarded as having inherent powers. It was said to have been created on the sixth day, i.e. the day when all the most important creations were made. It was given to Adam, and descended through Enoch, Shem, Abraham, Isaac, Jacob, Joseph, and then to Pharaoh, from whom Jethro stole it and planted it in his garden. Jethro then promised to give his daughter Zipporah in marriage to the man who could pull it out of the earth. As it was inscribed with the Ineffable Name this was impossible until Moses, who knew the Name, was successful. It was made of the wood of the Tree of Life, and later became the transverse beam of the Cross. When the Israelites, having defeated the Amorites, were preparing to attack Moab, Balak, king of Moab[3], sent in haste to the great magician Balaam, son of Beor, king of Edom, for help. The ritual for the magical dispersal of the enemy is given in full detail, but the omens being against success in battle, Balak and Balaam abandoned the attempt to overwhelm the enemy by magic. King David had his own private seer[4] to whom he turned for advice in any difficult situation. It will be seen then that magicians were in high favour at royal courts, and that even a king might be a diviner and foreteller of the future. At a much later date the celebrated College of Augurs in Rome shows that the diviner was still held in the utmost respect, and that the importance of the magician was not diminished.

Contemporary documentary evidence of the religion and priesthoods of Britain before the Roman occupation is rare. Caesar's hurried visits gave him time to note only some of the most dramatic ritual. Though he had only surface knowledge, he has at least recorded that the priesthood, whom he calls the Druids, were foretellers of the future and were held in high honour. As the Britons were entirely illiterate, it was not until the coming of the Christian monks and missionaries that there is any real account of the Paganism of this country. Even then it must be remembered that the accounts were written by highly prejudiced observers. Yet they could not belittle the importance of that great prophet and magician, Merlin, Pagan though he was.

According to the legend, Merlin was the son of a nun and the Devil, i.e. the pre-Christian God. It is possible that the 'nun' was in reality a Pagan holy woman or priestess, of the type later stigmatized as a witch. Merlin would thus be one of those many magical children born of God and a human mother, and would owe his knowledge of the magic arts to his early training from his witch mother. The belief in his prophetic power had an influence far exceeding that of the Bible, for the Bible was a new and exotic book in a foreign language, whereas Merlin's prophecies were in the vernacular and were passed from one to another of the people by word of mouth. Merlin's prophecies refer only to the royal family, and were continually quoted by all classes in the kingdom. They must therefore be taken into consideration in any study of the beliefs prevalent in Plantagenet, Tudor, and Stuart times.

In 1120 the White Ship was wrecked, and Henry I lost his only son, his illegitimate daughter, and his niece. This tragedy was believed to have been foretold by Merlin in the words, 'The Lion's whelps shall be transformed into fishes of the sea.'⁵ Merlin was quoted and implicitly believed as late as the middle of the seventeenth century. Charles II was born in 1630. 'At the birth of this Prince on May 29th, Merlin's prophecy was fulfilled, for there appeared a star about one o'clock in the afternoon, the very time of his birth, when the King rode to St. Paul's to give thanks to God for her Majesty's being safely delivered of a son. Some said it was Mercury, Merlin having said, the splendour of the sun shall languish by the paleness of Mercury, and it shall be dreadful to all beholders.'⁶

The ancient Kelts always had a prophet-magician attached to the army, whose business it was to make incantations for victory and to lead the soldiers in battle. This was an important and highly coveted position, and after the conversion to Christianity was usually filled by a prominent Christian saint. The Irish Saint Findchua was called upon to exert his powers when Meath was attacked by an enemy. 'The cleric's nature rose against them, so that sparks of blazing fire burst forth from his teeth.' Roaring incantations he led the men of Meath into battle and annihilated the enemy.[7] On another occasion the King of Leinster found that the Druid, whose business it was, was too old to lead the army into battle, he therefore sent for Findchua, who undertook the task. 'Then a prophetic fury seized him, "a wave of Godhead" it is termed; and he thundered forth a metrical incantation. The result was that victory declared for the men of Leinster.'[8] The metrical incantation or spell was obviously the work of a bard, and the curse of an Irish poet 'was no mere expression of opinion, but was a most potent weapon of war, which might blister an adversary's face or even cost him his life.'[9]

The Christian Church was organized in Rome when the status of women had so declined that the wife was merely the chattel of the husband. Therefore when the New Religion reached western Europe, women were strictly excluded from the priesthood. It followed then that a 'priestess', one who performed the sacred offices for the people in general, was a Pagan; and to a truly Christian bishop, priest, or monk, a Pagan was a devil-worshipper, given over to every kind of wickedness and debauchery. No epithet was too strong to be applied to them, they were witches, traffickers with the Devil, workers with evil spirits, and consequently accursed of God, the Christian God. But if the Pagan priestess could be masked with a thin veneer of Christianity, then she became a prophetess whose prayers were answered by the Almighty. It was not uncommon for priestesses, i.e. witches, to influence a battle, and here again the Christian saint is found taking the place of the witch. The King of Leinster took St. Brigid with him on one such occasion; he held her staff, while she cursed the enemy with so much vigour that they were completely routed.[10] St. Itha also successfully cursed the enemies of her chieftain before a battle.

These instances show that the Christian priest or saint was merely the successor of the Pagan priest and priestess, without any change except in the name of the god they invoked. The truth of the records is confirmed by the action of St. Augustine, who, when he 'converted' England placed bishops where there had been flamens, and archbishops where there had been archflamens. In other words, he kept the organization of the ancient religion, as well as the powers of the holders of those positions, without changing more than the name of the God and the title of the office. But in the eyes of the recorders, who were all Christians, these changes made all the difference, the Christian magician was a prophet, the Pagan magician was a witch.

There are many examples of the prophetic powers of the Saxon saints. In 685 Ecgfrith of Northumbria set out to do battle against the Picts; 'the divine Cuthbert, from his knowledge of future events, had both attempted to keep him back when departing, and at the very moment of his death, enlightened by heavenly influence, declared, though at a distance, that he was slain.'[11] St. Guthlac made two prophecies about Aethelbald of Mercia; the first was that he should be king, which came to pass.[12] The second was that he should be slain in battle, which Ingulph says came true, 'according to the prophecy of the holy father Guthlac.'[13] Unfortunately for the success of this prophecy, other and better recorders, such as Bede and Roger of Hoveden, relate that Aethelbald was 'murdered by his own people'.[14]

The most successful and renowed prophet of the Saxon period was St. Dunstan, Abbot of Glastonbury and Archbishop of Canterbury. He, however, appears to have been rivalled on occasion by Elfgiva, the mother of King Edgar, who was an interpreter of dreams, 'to whom God made many revelations'.[15] Dunstan's prophecies were many. I quote here only a few. When King Edgar was born, Dunstan heard an angelic voice saying, 'Peace be to England as long as this child shall reign and our Dunstan survive.'[16] When King Edmund was killed by the robber Leofa in 946, 'Dunstan at that time abbot of Glastonbury, had foreseen his ignoble end, being fully persuaded of it from the gesticulations and insolent mockery of a devil dancing before him.'[17] Again, when King Edred fell ill, 'Dunstan, learning by a messenger that he was sick, while urging his horse in order to see him, heard a voice thundering over his head, "Now King Edred sleeps in the Lord".'[18] Dunstan also prophesied the death of Editha, daughter of King Edgar. 'Soon shall this blooming rose wither; soon shall this beloved bird take flight to God, after the expiration of six weeks from this time. . . . On the appointed day, this noble lady expired in her prime, at the age of twenty-three years.'[19] In 979 at the coronation of Ethelred the Unready, Dunstan prophesied that 'such evils shall come upon the English nation as they have never suffered from the time they came to England until now.'[20]

The Norman period shows the practice of a court prophet, though he seems to have been occasionally distinct from the Christian priest or prelate. The archbishops were now almost invariably foreigners, and it is possible that the quarrels between king and bishops may have arisen from a difference of opinion as to some of the functions of the successor of an archflamen. But as William the Conqueror had his own private astrologer these differences did not arise. The violent storm which occurred when he crossed the Channel to take possession of England, resulted in the loss of two of his ships, in one of which was his astrologer. The loss, however, did not affect the issue of the battle of Hastings. Yet William evidently still believed in the efficacy of charms and incantations in battle, for when he went against Hereward the Wake at Ely he employed a witch to use direful incantations and curses against the enemy.[21] William Rufus was apparently a firm disbeliever in any prophecy made by a Christian priest. 'The devil appeared visibly and expressed to men of the sudden death of King William. King William monished thereof set not thereby.'[22] On the very day of

Rufus's death, Robert fitz Hamon, a friend of the king, received a visit from a monk, who reported that he had dreamed a dreadful dream the previous night; he had seen Rufus enter a church and tear the crucifix to pieces. 'The image at length struck the king with its foot in such a manner that he fell backwards; from his mouth, as he lay prostrate, issued so copious a flame that the volumes of smoke touched the very stars.' Fitz-Hamon was alarmed, and related the dream to the king. 'William, repeatedly laughing, exclaimed, "He is a monk, and dreams for money like a monk; give him a hundred shillings".'[23]

Under the Plantagenets there were many similar incidents recorded. King John, however, was like Rufus in holding all such so-called supernatural prophecies in contempt, and in 1212 he dealt drastically with such a prophet. 'A certain Peter of Pontefract prophesied that after the king had reigned prosperously for fourteen years, neither he nor his heirs should rule any more; and this was believed by his hearers as if the words had been spoken by a voice from heaven', and the day was actually fixed on which the reign should come to an end. John took action at once. 'He caused to be drawn and hanged at London, one Piers of Pomfret, for the said Peter had monished divers mishaps that should come to him for his vicious life, and also for he had often warned King John that he should reign but 14 years.'[24] It is possible that the unpopularity of both Rufus and John among the priestly chroniclers was due to the firm disbelief of both these kings in all ecclesiastical prophecies of evil. Henry VIII dealt in the same drastic manner and for the same reason with Elizabeth Barton and her coadjutors in 1533.[25]

Priests were not the only astrologers, for one of Edward I's contemporaries, King Robert of Sicily, 'was much renowned as a great astrologer, and full of deep sciences; he had often cast the nativities of the kings of France and England, and had found, by his astrology and the influence of the stars, that, if the king of France fought with the king of England in person, he would surely be defeated.'[26]

Rain-makers. The ritual of the Old Religion, as disclosed in the trials of the witches, shows that much of the worship of the Pagans was for the increase of fertility. When agriculture became as important as animal husbandry the priest or priestess claimed to be able to induce the Deity to produce or withhold rain as required for the crops. In short, the priesthood were the rain-makers.

One of the earliest examples on record of a rain-maker is the prophet Samuel,[27] who on two occasions called up a heavy thunderstorm. The first time was to disperse the Philistine army, but the second occasion was from sheer personal vanity to prove to the people that, though he was old, his magical power was not diminished. The lives of early Christian saints show various examples of the power of priests and holy women over the weather. The same power belonged to the witches.

As Henry IV was regarded by large numbers of the people as a mere usurper, omens and spells against him were eagerly recorded. He appears to have been peculiarly unlucky in the weather, so much so that many were convinced it was a case of witchcraft.

> *The king had never but tempest foul and rain,*
> *As long as he ay in Walēs ground;*
> *Rocks and mists, winds and storms ever certain;*
> *All men trowed that witches made that stound.*[28]

All the omens and prognostications were so against him that it was certain his ill-luck would descend to his heirs.

> *For when Henry the fourth first was crowned,*
> *Many a wiseman said then full commonly,*
> *The third heir should not joice, but be uncrowned,*
> *And deposed of all regality.*[29]

The mists, which so aided Edward IV at the great Battle of Barnet, when the Lancastrian forces were finally defeated, were said to have been raised by a monk. 'Of the mists and other impediments which fell upon the lords' party, by reason of the incantations wrought by Friar Bungay, as the fame went, me list not to write.[30]

It is an interesting fact that when Anne Boleyn was arrested by the Lieutenant of the Tower and brought by water through Traitor's Gate, she told him as she landed that there would be no rain in England until she left the Tower.[31] This remark suggests that she at least believed that she possessed certain magical powers.

The most remarkable case of the storm-raising powers of the witches was at North Berwick in 1590, when under the command of Francis, Lord Bothwell, three covens by means of a 'conjuring of cats' claimed to have raised so great a storm that James VI and his bride were nearly wrecked when coming from Oslo to Leith. The cat was christened and given a Christian name (Margaret), the joints of a dead man were tied to its feet, and it was cast into the sea with the shout of 'Hola, Satan!'[32]

One of the most surprising magical ceremonies performed at the English court was when James I lay on his deathbed. The ceremony was obviously to transfer the pain from which the king was suffering, to an animal, and is the only complete account of the rite. The animal was a gryse (young pig) which was dressed like a baby, one of the court ladies acted as the mother, the Duchess of Buckingham was dressed as the midwife (always an important person at a christening), a gentleman of the court dressed as a bishop read the baptismal service from a prayer-book, while the Duke of Buckingham and other gentlemen acted as godfathers. When the ceremony was over, the pig was released and chased out of the room.[33] When later the duke was accused of taking part in a blasphemous performance, he said it was done only to make the king laugh. But as the Duchess was known to be a 'witch', it would seem to have been a magical rite to relieve suffering.

The methods of Foretelling the future were very varied. Prognostications could be made from natural phenomena. The Norman Conquest was 'presaged by the threatening brilliance of a large comet of a bloody colour with long hair.'³⁴ The anonymous author of the *Acts of King Stephen* gives a vivid account of what was probably a fine display of the aurora borealis, which occured just before a devastating raid of the Scotch into Northumberland. 'A large quarter of the heavens was seen to emit fiery sparks like a furnace, and balls of fire of a wonderful brightness shot through the air. This visible appearance of a flaming sky portended either a great effusion of blood, which speedily followed, or the burning of towns and villages. . . . Let not the reader taunt me with telling an idle tale when I say, that having myself witnessed the hemisphere in a flame, and seen with my own eyes luminous flakes floating densely in the blazing sky, I considered these portents to be the precursers of coming evils, and to portend that dreadful scourge, which soon afterwards devastated Northumberland.'³⁵

The two kings, who died by bloodshed and narrowly escaped canonization, were Henry VI and Charles I, and omens as to their fate were numerous. When Henry VI was forced to appoint the Duke of York as his heir, two omens occurred which appear to have impressed all those who witnessed them. 'The commons of the realm being assembled in the common house, coming and treating upon the title of the said duke of York, suddenly fell down the crown which hung then in the midst of the said house, which was taken for a prodigy or token that the reign of king Harry was ended: and also the crown which stood on the highest tower of the steeple in the castle of Dover fell down the same year.'³⁶ Polydore Vergil, recording the scene in the House of Commons, says that Henry was 'in his robes royal' and that the crown fell from his head.³⁷

The first of the terrible omens which foretold the fate of Charles I was when the Knight Marshal was proclaiming him as king, for, instead of calling him 'the rightful and indubitable heir', he made a slip and called him 'rightful and dubitable heir'. Though the Knight Marshal was at once corrected by his secretary, the mistake had been made and was promptly noted. When Charles opened his first Parliament, he wore his crown, though he had not yet been crowned, this also was noted as an evil omen. When he was actually on his way to Whitehall for his coronation, the blood of a wounded falcon fell on the neck of the bust of the king; and for the coronation sermon the Bishop of Carlisle had chosen for his text the words, 'Be thou faithful unto death.'[43] And another omen pointed in the same direction, that he had been chief mourner three times, for his father, for his brother, and for his mother.[38]

An ordinary method of learning the future and of discovering secret events of the past was by raising the Devil. Though this method is recorded with horror, it appears to have been in frequent use. When Edmund, Duke of Kent, was uncertain whether his brother Edward II was alive or dead—the king's death having been kept secret—he raised the Devil who assured him that Edward was really dead.[39]

Two methods of divination survive to the present day, both were once religious rites, which to be effective had to be performed by the magician or priestess. The first of these was by casting either on the ground or on a prepared surface a number of small sacred objects, and judging by their position in regard to one another and by which surface of the thrown objects is uppermost. This is the method of Casting Lots so frequently mentioned in the Bible. The belief being that God directed the throw so that the objects indicated His will. The religious nature of the ceremony is seen by the fact that the breastplate of the Jewish Highpriest was used with Urim and Thummim, which were sacred objects kept in the temple and consulted only on occasions of peculiar importance. The method of casting lots was used to decide which of two candidates should fill the place of Judas Iscariot in the band of Apostles. It was probably a common method among the laity for deciding on some choice or course of action, as is still done by the toss and fall of a coin.

The other method was by scrying or crystal-gazing. This

is first recorded in the Bible in the story of Joseph when Benjamin was accused of stealing Joseph's silver cup, 'in which my lord drinketh and whereby he divineth.'[40] But it is not until a much later date that the method of divination by the bowl or cup is described. The bowl was of either black bronze or silver blackened inside; it had the figure of Anubis engraved on the bottom. It was filled with water, and a little fine oil was floated over the water; the object seems to have been to obtain a reflecting surface, bright but without glitter. The seer was usually a young boy under puberty; the magician or priest stood by, burning incense and reciting prayers and charms in a monotonous chant. The boy was then told to describe what he saw in the bowl, on which he kept his eyes fixed. He would first describe the coming of Anubis, who prepares royal thrones and a pavilion for the great gods; these finally enter in royal state; and being enthroned they answer the questions put to them by the priestly magician.[41]

This is an interesting method, for the detail enables one to fill in the blanks in the account of the Witch of Endor.[42] Saul was in great straits, he was on the eve of a battle against a powerful enemy and could obtain no divine guidance, for 'the Lord answered him not, neither by dreams, nor by Urim, nor by prophets.' In despair he reverted to the ancient method which he had so zealously tried to eradicate, and went in disguise with two attendants to one of the few diviners still left. The witch asked him whom he wished to speak with, and he answered 'Samuel'. The sequel shows that the witch now followed the ritual of the bowl. Saul asked what she saw, and she replied, 'Gods ascending out of the earth.' And then, 'An old man cometh up; and he is covered with a mantle.' It is clear that Saul saw nothing, and the witch's description might have fitted any important person, but Saul having wanted Samuel believed it was Samuel. It is possible that Saul, weak from fasting and in a highly nervous condition, imagined the words of the prophecy; but it is also possible that the woman was taking her revenge on the man who had massacred her co-religionists.

This method of divining is still in use in Morocco and other parts of the Mediterranean area. Black ink is poured into the palm of a young boy, who gazes into the ink-pool while the diviner intones the appropriate prayers. Presently the boy sees servants setting up a royal pavilion, they prepare a throne, and spread carpets. Then the Sultan in royal attire enters with many attendants; he seats himself on the throne and answers the questions put to him. This method, though usually employed to foretell the future, can also be used to identify a thief. Crystal-gazing is performed by means of a plain glass ball with a smooth surface. Here again the object on which the seer fixes his eyes is like the ink-pool and the oil and water in a black bowl, it has a reflecting surface without glitter. Dr. John Dee possessed a 'magic glass', which was a disc of highly polished cannel coal, in which he claimed to see angels and spirits.[43]

In every religion the priest or priestess wears special vestments when performing the sacred rites. The origin of the custom is probably due to the fear of 'the contagion of holiness', therefore garments worn in the immediate presence of the Deity had to be of some washing material, such as the linen vestments of the Egyptian and Jewish priests, or of some more elaborately decorated robes to be worn over the ordinary dress and discarded before leaving the sacred precincts. The effect of a holy object is recorded in the Old Testament in the account of what the captured Ark of the Lord did to the Philistines and also to its own people when returned to Beth Shemesh. The belief still survives in the generally accepted idea that anything taken from a sacred building, whether Christian church or Pagan temple, will bring bad luck.

A description of a northern witch's ceremonial dress occurs in the saga of Thorfinn Carlsemne.[44] She had a black mantle with clasps and set with precious stones right down to the skirts thereof. She had on her neck a string of glass beads, and on her head a hood of black lambskin lined with white catskin. She had a staff in her hand, and there was a knob on it; it was mounted with brass and set with stones round the knob. She had about her a girdle made of puff-balls strung together, and on it was a great skin pouch, in which she kept the charms needed for her magic. She had calfskin shoes, with the hair on, with long and strong thongs on them, and great knobs of latten on the side thereof. She had on her hands gloves of catskin, white and hairy inside.'*

There is some evidence that the early men-witches wore garments of dark blue, with dark blue caps; probably like the summer dress of the Lapps; for the whole Lapp nation, men, women, and children, were in medieval times regarded as witches and endued with evil magical powers. In the sixteenth century the men-witches had adopted garments of a more elaborate and startling type. 'Magicians as is well known were very curious in the choice and form of their vestments. Their caps are oval, or like pyramids, with lappets on each side, and fur within. Their gowns are long, and furred with fox-skins, under which they have a linen garment reaching to the knee. Their girdles are three inches broad, and have many cabalistic names, with crosses, trines, and circles, inscribed on them. Their shoes should be of new russet leather, with a cross cut upon them. Their knives are dagger fashion, and their swords have neither guard nor scabbard.'[45]

* It is interesting to note that by the Synod of Westminster in 1127 abbesses and nuns (who as holy women were the Christian counterparts of the Pagan priestess or witch), were forbidden to wear any other fur than lambs-wool or catskin.—*Florence of Worcester*, p. 244, ed. Bohn.

The Divine Victim

'It is expedient that one man should die for the people.'—JOHN xi. 50.

There is a strong body of evidence to show that in the primitive cult of western Europe the god was sacrificed. The Christian inquisitors are unanimous on this point, and the direct accounts given at the trials of the witches confirm their statements.

In countries where such sacrifices were offered there were three methods of killing the victim: (1) by fire, the ashes being scattered on the fields or thrown into running water, (2) by shedding of blood so that the blood should actually fall on the ground, (3) by some form of asphyxiation; in this case the body was either dismembered and the fragments buried in the fields, or was burnt and the ashes scattered. The incarnate god was originally the king or chief of the tribe, later his place was taken by a substitute, who was often for a time allowed the status and insignia of royalty. Mock kings, who were put to death at the end of a given term, are a well-known feature of early religions.

The underlying meaning of the sacrifice of the divine victim is that the spirit of God takes up its abode in a human being, usually the king, who thereby becomes the giver of fertility to all his kingdom. When the divine man begins to show signs of age he is put to death lest the spirit of God should also grow old and weaken like its human container. But until the time of sacrifice arrives no sacrilegious hand may be raised against the incarnate god; for his death, by accident or design, means overwhelming disaster to the people. When, however, the time comes for him to die no

16a. PUCK FAIR PROCESSION

(By courtesy of the 'Cork Examiner')

16b. CROWNING OF THE PUCK KING

(By courtesy of the 'Cork Examiner')

hand may be outstretched to save him. In some places the
time of death was indicated by signs of approaching age,
such as grey hair or loss of teeth; in other places a term of
years was fixed, usually either seven or nine. When the
changes inevitable to all human customs gradually took place,
a substitute could suffer in the king's stead, dying at the
time the king should have died and thus giving the king a
further lease of life.

This, put shortly, is the theory and cult of the Dying God.
The belief belongs to all parts of the Old World, and survives
in Africa into the present century. It was a fundamental
dogma of the pre-Christian religion of Europe, believed in
and practised as ardently as among the Africans of to-day.

To investigate the subject of the Divine Victim of the
Witch-cult it is essential to put aside all preconceived ideas,
remembering always that the records were made by the prejudiced pens of monkish chroniclers. The subject must be
approached with the same unbiased mind as though the
religion under investigation belonged to ancient Egypt or
to modern savages. That the sacrifice was repeatedly consummated within the historic period of our own country and
of France depends upon evidence which would be accepted
if it were offered in respect of an Oriental or African religion.

There are indications that in England the sacrifice took
place every seven years; in Normandy, Scandinavia, and
France every nine years. In the seven-year cycle King
Edmund was stabbed at Pucklechurch in May, 946; in
November, 1016, Edmund Ironside was done to death,
according to some authorities by a vote of the Witan, and
like Rufus the mode of death was by an arrow: in August,
1100, Rufus fell in the New Forest. In all these instances
the month is noticeable as being one in which one of the
four great Sabbaths was held.

In the nine-year cycle the month is apparently of no importance. Here the evidence is chiefly from France and
Scandinavia. A traditional king of Sweden is said to have
sacrificed a substitute every nine years until the ninth had

been offered up; he died at an advanced age before it was time to sacrifice the tenth. In 792, Osred, king of Northumbria, was put to death. In 1035, Cnut died or was murdered. In 1080, Walchere, bishop of Durham, was slain by the people at the gate of his own church. It is worth noting that he was from Lorraine, Joan of Arc's country, and that when he was conducted to Winchester to be consecrated, queen Edgitha remarked, 'We have here a noble martyr.' In 1431, Joan of Arc perished at the stake; in 1440, Gilles de Rais was hanged. At the intersection of the two cycles, in 1170, Thomas à Becket was murdered at Canterbury.

I now bring forward the evidence for regarding four well-known historical personages as Divine Victims; William Rufus, Thomas à Becket, Joan of Arc, and Gilles de Rais. The Church has canonized two and execrated two, but the records show that in all four cases there are underlying factors suppressed by the Christian chroniclers, which must be sought for in order to explain the otherwise inexplicable events.

William Rufus[1]

In the case of William Rufus it is only by realizing that all the factors were not recorded by the Christian chroniclers that any explanation of his character or the events of his life and death can be obtained. Freeman, having no anthropological knowledge, is entirely biased by the ecclesiastical point of view, and acknowledges himself totally unable to understand the character of Rufus or to explain many of the events of his reign. If, however, it is granted that Rufus was not a Christian but a professed Pagan, his character becomes quite consistent, and his life and death are in keeping with his religion.

By ancestry, Rufus came of a Pagan stock which regarded the king as a deity (or devil, if the Christian phraseology is used). It is recorded that at the end of the tenth century or beginning of the eleventh, the Devil, in the likeness of the

Duke of Normandy, came to the Duke's wife in a wood, and as the result of the union she bore a son who was known as Robert the Devil. There was nothing in Robert's character to warrant such an appellation if the word had an evil connotation; but if, as I maintain, the Chief or king were regarded as God Incarnate among the Normans, the son of the king would become on accession both king and god. It would be entirely consonant with the usual Christian practice to stigmatize the heathen divinity as the Devil even when in human form, and the belief that the old god was the enemy of the new would account for the use of the epithet. The son of Robert the Devil was William the Conqueror, who married his cousin Matilda, therefore on both his father's and his mother's side Rufus descended from a Pagan chief or Devil.

Rufus's favourite oath was 'Per vultum de Luca', usually translated as 'By the face of Lucca'. It was the oath he always used when he threatened or promised; when, in short, he meant what he said. In that long-drawn-out struggle of wills between Rufus and the Bishop of Durham, Rufus is recorded as using the oath twice. The matter at issue was whether the king was supreme in his own kingdom, or whether the Pope had the right to interfere. The Bishop refused to surrender his castle, till Rufus said, 'By the face of Lucca, you shall never go out of my hands till I have your castle.' Knowing that the threat would be fulfilled, the Bishop yielded the castle. Later on Rufus demanded that the Bishop should give sureties that Robert, Duke of Normandy, would not send ships to invade England during the king's absence. In vain the Bishop pleaded that he could not be answerable for another man; 'the irate king said, "By the Face of Luca, you shall not cross the sea this year unless you give the required surety for the ships." ' Again the Bishop found it advisable to yield.

Eadmer, who was contemporary with Rufus, records that when the king was pressed by bishops and priests to appoint an Archbishop, Rufus declared: 'By the holy Face of Lucca (for thus he was wont to swear), he and any other who would be archbishop may this time give place to me, for I will be archbishop myself.' Eadmer gives an interesting variant of the oath in his account of the curious incident of the discussion of their respective religions by a Christian and a Jew, which Rufus arranged in order that he should be able to judge whether the Jew's son, who had recently become a Christian, should remain in his new faith or return to the faith of his father. He decided that the young man should return to his original religion or be put to death. To all remonstrances he turned a deaf ear, saying, 'By the Face of God (*per vultum dei*), if you do not condemn him according to my will, I will condemn you.'

The uncritical equation of *Luce* with the town of Lucca is due to the unique variant of the oath given by Gervase of Tilbury (*circa* 1211) as 'vultus Lucanus', which is explained by a story of the Veronica type, that when the body of Christ was taken down from the cross Nicodemus spread a cloth over the dead face, which was then miraculously printed on the fabric. The evidence of Eadmer, who was a contemporary of Rufus, is surely to be preferred to that of Gervase, who lived rather more than a century later. Eadmer's variant 'dei' for 'de Luce' shows that Luce (Luca, Luci) is a name for God, though whether the Christian or a Pagan deity is not indicated. The greatest oaths have always been by the Almighty, never by God in human form, whose status and powers are, consciously or unconsciously, regarded as inferior. Rufus, as a Pagan, would hardly swear by a miraculous portrait of a God in whom he did not believe, preserved in an obscure town in a country which he must have connected with a foreign religion; a religion to which he did not belong, and whose officers he either disliked or despised. But Rufus, as a Pagan, had a God of his own, in all probability one whom his ancestors had worshipped. Among the great gods of the Norse-men was Loki, whose name could well be latinized as 'Luce' or 'Luca'. The legends of Loki show that he was originally one of the supreme gods of the Norse-men; and though, under the impact of new ideas and the usual changes in human affairs, he was finally regarded as evil, this was the fate common to all highly-placed deities, for 'the God of the Old Religion becomes the Devil of the New.' 'By the Face of Loki' would be an appropriate oath for a Norse-man.

Many of the Red King's friends and intimates were openly heathen or had merely the thinnest veneer of Christianity. His chief adviser was Randolf Flambard, the son of a Pagan woman, or 'witch' as the priestly chroniclers called her.

As regards the character of Rufus, which Freeman acknowledges he cannot estimate, it displays all the Pagan virtues. Rufus was a dutiful son, an able and competent ruler, a faithful friend, a generous enemy, recklessly courageous, lavishly openhanded, and was never known to break his plighted word. The Church accused him of immorality, but unlike his Christian father and his Christian brothers he left no illegitimate children. He had the savagery of his period, but he never killed with that fiendish refinement of cruelty which marked Henry I's treatment of Conan; but as Henry was professedly a Christian and always favoured the Church his faults and sins were condoned and glossed over by the monkish historians. Yet Ordericus Vitalis, monk though he was and prejudiced by his Christianity, sums up the character of William II in a manner which shows the king as a great man and a fine ruler: 'Rufus was imperious, daring and warlike, and gloried in the pomp of his numerous troops. The king's memory was very tenacious, and his zeal for good or evil was ardent. Robbers and thieves felt the terrible weight of his power, and his efforts to keep the peace throughout his dominion were unceasing. He so managed his subjects, either by making them partakers of his bounty or curbing them by the terror of his arms, that no one dared whisper a word in opposition to his will.' Rufus compares favourably with any of his contemporaries, more especially with his father and brothers. It is clear therefore that the antagonism he aroused in the priestly chroniclers was due to some cause other than his personal character.

The Divine Victim

It is customary also to speak with bated breath of the 'awful' death of Rufus, but if the account of his death and burial are compared with those of his father the 'awfulness' will be found to belong to the passing of the Christian, rather than of the Pagan, king. The monkish writers make much of the fact that Rufus met his death in the New Forest, and affect to regard it as a judgment upon him for destroying for his own pleasure villages and churches, great stress being, of course, laid on the destruction of the churches. But the chroniclers conveniently forgot that it was the Christian Conqueror who made the Forest, and that it was his equally Christian son, Henry I, who strengthened the Conqueror's game-laws and stringently enforced them. If death in the New Forest were really a judgment of God for the destruction of churches, it was the Conqueror who should have died there and not Rufus.

The first surprising event in the career of Rufus was his reception as king by the English. That the son of the savage Conqueror, who had so recently devastated the land, should be accepted whole-heartedly by the people needs some explanation. The Conqueror's dying bequest would have had no weight, and Lanfranc was important only in a restricted circle. If however Rufus belonged to the Old Religion his position becomes clear. Lanfranc gained from him a promise to respect the Church during his (Lanfranc's) lifetime; and it has always been remarked that Rufus not only kept this promise but throughout his life he never interfered with any benefactions which his father had made to Christian foundations. On Lanfranc's death Rufus was no longer bound by his promise; and, as Freeman puts it, 'one aspect of the reign of William Rufus sets him before us as the enemy, almost the persecutor, of the Church in his realm.'

The stories told of Rufus bear all the marks of truth and show him as definitely a Pagan. He jeered openly at Christianity, delighting to set Jews and Christians to discuss the merits of their respective religions; he plundered churches and religious establishments, 'have ye not chests full of bones of dead men, but wrought about with gold and silver', said one of his ministers to the monks who protested that they had no money for the king. Rufus openly declared that neither Saint Peter nor any other saint had any influence with God, and he would ask none of them for help. One of the accusations against Rufus was that he had the temerity to disbelieve in the ordeal. When fifty deer-stealers had cleared themselves by this means, Rufus said that God either did not know the deeds of men or else he weighed them in an unfair balance. He was also wroth if anyone ventured to add the usual reserve of 'God's will' to anything that he (Rufus) undertook or ordered to be undertaken. He had that belief in himself that he would have everything referred to his wisdom and power only. This is quite consistent if Rufus believed himself to be God Incarnate.

Our knowledge of Rufus is obtained chiefly from Christian chroniclers, at whose hands the character of a heathen king would receive scant justice. How far such chronicles may be trusted can be seen by comparing the portrait of Randolf Flambard as drawn by the priestly writers of southern England with that shown by the monks of Durham. In the hands of the southerners he is a monster of wickedness, without a redeeming feature, while the northerners represent him as a meek and holy saint. In England Rufus has been recorded only by those men who also vilified Flambard, but in Normandy his deeds were acclaimed by poets who were not ecclesiastics and who might not even have been Christians. The whole story of Rufus has been presented to the modern reader from the records of his bitter enemies.

The accounts of his death are varied though all agree that he was killed by an arrow shot by one of his own people while he was hunting in the New Forest. It is clear that his death was expected, and the account of his last hours indicates that he knew his time had come. He could not sleep during the previous night, and he ordered lights to be brought into his bed-chamber and made his chamberlains

enter and talk with him. All the forenoon of that fatal day
he occupied himself with serious business, and how well he
did this is shown by the fact that there was no confusion or
loss of time in the appointment and crowning of his successor. His business being ended, he went to his dinner,
when he ate and drank more than usual. He then began to
array himself for his last ride, and while his boots were being
laced a smith brought him six new arrows for use with the
cross-bow. The king took them joyfully and gave two to
Walter Tyrrel, saying significantly, 'It is right that the
sharpest arrows should be given to him who knows how to
deal deadly strokes with them.' There came at this moment
a letter from Abbot Serlo urging the king not to go hunting
as one of the monks had had a warning dream that such an
expedition meant death. Rufus merely laughed and made a
sarcastic remark about 'snoring monks', but with his usual
lavish generosity sent the dreamer a handsome present in
money. He then turned to Tyrrel with another significant
remark, 'Walter, do thou do justice according to those things
which thou hast heard.' Tyrrel answered with equal significance, 'So I will, my lord.'

In the Forest the king dismounted and stood with Tyrrel
waiting for the deer to pass. The usual story is that the king
shot and missed, then Tyrrel loosed his arrow which glanced
off the stag's antlers or off the branch of a tree and pierced
the king's heart. The most vivid account is from William
of Malmesbury, who says that it was late in the afternoon,
'the sun was now declining, when the king, drawing his bow
and letting fly an arrow, slightly wounded a stag; and keenly
gazing followed it, still running, a long time with his eyes,
holding up his hand to keep off the power of the sun's rays.'
Walter then shot at another stag and by mischance the arrow
pierced the king. 'On receiving the wound the king uttered
not a word; but breaking off the shaft of the weapon where
it projected from his body, fell upon the wound by which
he accelerated his death.' Knighton's version is also dramatic;
and if the words attributed to Rufus are true they convey

the idea that the killing was premeditated and that Rufus was aware that his end was at hand. He was shooting at a stag and his bowstring broke; he called to Tyrrel to shoot, but Tyrrel hesitated. Then Rufus burst out, 'Draw, draw your bow for the Devil's sake and let fly your arrow, or it will be the worse for you' (*Trahe, trahe arcum ex parte diaboli, et extende sagittam, alias te poenitebit*).

The body, according to the ecclesiastical account, was found by a charcoal burner. It was placed on a rough cart, covered with a poor ragged cloak and conveyed for burial to Winchester. William of Malmesbury makes a great point of the blood dripping to the earth during the whole journey; though this is an actual impossibility the record is consistent with the belief that the blood of the Divine Victim must fall on the ground to fertilize it. Malmesbury notes that Rufus was mourned by few of the nobles and ecclesiastics who attended his funeral, but Ordericus records that the poor, the widows, the mendicants, went out to meet the funeral procession and followed the dead king to his grave. This fact alone shows that to the common people he had been a just ruler and that they knew they had lost a friend, it also suggests that the peasantry were still Pagan and mourned their dead god.

The Norman accounts of the finding and burial of the body were written by poets, not priests. The lamentations of the nobles, who wept and tore their hair, are first described; then follows the making of the bier, which was strewn with flowers and slung between two richly harnessed palfreys. A baron's mantle was spread on the bier, and on this the king's body was laid, and another rich mantle was laid over him. With mourning and grief the procession went to Winchester, where they were received by nobles, clergy, bishops, and abbots. The next day was the burial, when for him monk and clerk and abbot '*bien ont lu et bien chanté*'. Never had such a funeral been seen, never had so many masses been sung for any king as for him.

The death of Rufus was expected before it happened, and

was known within a few hours in Italy and in more than one place in England. In Belgium, Hugh, Abbot of Clugny, was warned the previous night that the king's life was at an end. On the day of the death Peter de Melvis in Devonshire met a rough common man bearing a bloody dart, who said to him, 'With this dart your king was killed to-day.' The same day the Earl of Cornwall, while walking in the woods, met a large black hairy goat carrying the figure of the king. On being questioned the goat replied that he was the Devil taking the king to judgment. Anselm received the news in Italy through a young and splendid man, who told the clerk on guard at Anselm's door that all dissension between the king and the archbishop was now at an end. A monk, of the Order to which Ordericus Vitalis belonged, had a vision very early in the morning after the death of Rufus; he was chanting in the church when he beheld through his closed eyes a person holding out a paper on which was written, 'King William is dead'; when he opened his eyes the person had vanished.

Though the stories are slightly childish they all suggest that the death was expected, and the news was probably signalled from one place to another. The most suggestive of the stories is that of the black goat, when it is remembered that this was the form in which the ancient god (in Christian parlance, the Devil) was wont to appear in France.

In the entire history of Rufus, more particularly in the stories of his death, it is clear that the whole truth is not given; something is kept back. If, however, Rufus was in the eyes of his subjects the God Incarnate, Man Divine, who died for his people, the Christian chroniclers would naturally not record a fact which to them would savour of blasphemy, and the Pagans, being illiterate, made no records.

The date of Rufus's death, August 2nd, seems significant; it is always emphatically called 'the morrow of Lammas'. Lammas, the 1st of August, was one of the four great Festivals of the Old Religion, and there is evidence to show that it was on the great Sabbaths only that the human sacrifice was offered. If then my theory is correct Rufus died as the Divine Victim in the seven-year cycle.

Thomas à Becket[2]

The death of Thomas à Becket presents many features which are explicable only by the theory that he also was the substitute for a Divine King. The relative position of King and Archbishop from Saxon times onward was so peculiar that it suggests a closer connection between the two offices than appears at first sight. The most remarkable instances are Edwy and Dunstan, William the Conqueror and Lanfranc, Rufus and Anselm, Henry II and Becket. The quarrels between king and archbishop were not always politico-religious, there was often a strong personal element; such bitter quarrels never occurred with the Archbishop of York, whose importance in the north was as great as that of Canterbury in the south. In the dissensions between Rufus and Anselm as well as in the disputes between Henry and Becket most of the bishops sided with the king. It is possible that, as wherever there had been a flamen of the Pagan religion a bishopric had been founded and an archbishop had replaced an arch-flamen, the duties of the arch-flamen of Canterbury descended to his Christian successor. If this were so, was perhaps one of those duties that the arch-flamen should act as the substitute for the king when a royal victim was required?

Though there is as yet no actual proof of this theory, certain facts go to support it. Dunstan's behaviour to Edwy was that of the mock king to the real king, as can be seen in innumerable instances where the mock king's actions are recorded. The stories of Dunstan's magical powers show that he was regarded by the people as having more than mortal qualities. He died on February 2nd, one of the four great quarterly Sabbaths. William I was not called upon for sacrifice, therefore Lanfranc's relations with the king were friendly; but it should be noted that the appointment to the see was entirely in the king's hands, and that Lanfranc accepted the post as a king's man. The bitter quarrels between Rufus and Anselm seem to owe their point to personal feeling. If the Pagan Rufus were prepared to fulfil the old custom of sacrifice, he might naturally desire a substitute. Anselm's persistent appeal to the Pope, though at first he had been content to accept his high position from Rufus, may mean that he refused to be the victim, perhaps from want of personal courage or because he would not consent to a Pagan custom, which in the end Rufus had to fulfil in his own person.

With Henry II and Becket there was the same conflict. Like Anselm, Becket was not supported by the greater number of his fellow-bishops, and like Anselm, also, he was driven out of the country by the king. But Henry was a sterner and more ruthless man than Rufus; and when Becket continued obstinate his kinsfolk were stripped of their possessions and driven into exile and Henry used all the means in his power to force Becket to surrender, and succeeded in the end. The last time that the two met was in Normandy, and when the archbishop mounted his horse to leave the king held the stirrup for him. This humility was not in accordance with Henry's character, but if Becket had consented to be the Divine Victim the real king would then, according to custom, be subordinate for the time being to the mock king.

That Becket was regarded as a Divine Victim is seen in the comparisons between his death and that of Christ, which are found in all the contemporary biographies, comparisons quite impossible if the death of the archbishop were simply murder. The monk, William of Canterbury, who was actually an eye-witness of the scene in Canterbury Cathedral, forces the parallel to an extraordinary extent: 'As the Lord, his passion being imminent, approached the place of suffering, so Thomas, aware of coming events, drew near to the place in which he should suffer. They sought to seize, as Jesus, so Thomas, but no one put a hand on him because his hour was not yet come. The Lord went in triumphal procession before His passion, Thomas before his. The Lord suffered after supper, and Thomas suffered after supper. The Lord for three days was guarded in Jerusalem by the Jews, Thomas for some days was guarded in the enclosure of his church. The Lord going to meet those who sought to attack Him, said, "I am he whom ye seek": Thomas to those who sought him, "Behold me." The Lord, "If ye seek me, let these depart"; Thomas, "Hurt none of those who stand by." That one there, this one here, was wounded. There four soldiers, here four soldiers. There the sharing of the garments, here of the mules. There the dispersion of the disciples, here the dispersion of the underlings. There the veil was rent, here the sword was broken. The Lord gave forth water and blood unto salvation; Thomas water and blood unto health. The Lord restored the lost world, Thomas recalled to life many lost ones.'

Like Rufus, Becket knew that his death was near and that it would be by violence; and, again as in the case of Rufus, monks dreamed of his approaching death. William of Canterbury says in the *Vita*, 'he knew that the sword threatened his head, and the time was at hand for his sacrifice.' This was on the 29th of December, the very day of the martyrdom, when Becket made his last confession to William of Maidstone. It is also noticeable in the quotation given above that it was acknowledged that his time was already fixed, 'for his hour was not yet come.' The knights' mocking words at the end seem to indicate that Becket had some claim to royal power.

The whole account of the murder is given by the eye-witness, William of Canterbury, who appears to have been a visitor at the monastery at the time. The scenes are vividly described; the violence of the knights, the perturbation of the frightened monks, their disorganized and ineffective attempts to save their chief, and the determination of Becket to be killed. After the first interview with the knights, the monks gathered round Becket and pushed him through the door, though he struggled against them. 'Thence gradually he progressed by slow degrees as if voluntarily courting death.' He saw the people assembled as if at a spectacle and asked what it was that they feared, and was told, 'Armed men in the cloisters.' At once he tried to force his way out, but was prevented by the monks who urged him to take refuge in the sanctuary of the cathedral. He fairly lost his temper when he saw them trying to bar the door. 'Go away,' he said, 'cowards! Let the miserable and the blind rave. We command you by virtue of your obedience not to shut the door!' The knights rushed in, and when they hesitated to begin Becket deliberately taunted them as if intending to make them lose control. He then bent his head, stretching out his neck that they might the more conveniently strike with their swords. After the first blow he fell face downwards, as though prostrate in prayer, and in that attitude was despatched. The terrified monks had fled to the altar fearing that every moment would be their last; but the knights had no enmity to them. They broke the arm of the English monk, Edward Grim, who defended Becket to the last, and another priest, who ran out evidently with some wild idea of giving help, was half stunned by a blow on the head with the flat of a sword, otherwise the flustered crowd at the altar received no hurt. The knights cried out mockingly, when the murder was consummated, 'He wished to be king, he wished to be more than king, just let him be king.'

The account continues with a description of the appearance of Becket's body after death. 'He did not seem to be dead, but by the vivid colour, the closed eyes and mouth, to be asleep. The limbs did not throb, no rigor of the body, no discharge issuing from the mouth or nostrils, nor was anything of the kind seen throughout the night by the watchers. But the flexibility of the fingers, the peace of the limbs, the cheerfulness and graciousness of the face, declared him a glorified man, even if his life and the cause of his passion had been silent.' This condition is not in accordance with the appearance of a body after death by the kind of wounds which killed Becket, but the miraculous condition of the body of a Divine Victim is commented on not only in the case of Becket but in the cases of Rufus and Joan of Arc. The body of Rufus dripped blood all the way to Winchester, though bleeding normally ceases soon after death. Joan's heart was found unconsumed and full of blood when the ashes were gathered up to be thrown into the river. In all three cases the miraculous element in the body after death is emphasized.

The ritual beating of the king after the death of his substitute was transformed by the Church into penance for the murder. Here the ritual flagellation was, as is always the case, severe enough to draw blood, so though the king was not killed his blood was shed.

As with Rufus, the death of Becket was known in many places on the same day on which it occurred or within a few hours of the event. At Argentan a voice was heard crying horribly, 'Behold, my blood cries from the ground to God more loudly than the blood of righteous Abel who was killed at the beginning of the world.' The very night of the murder the news was known in Jerusalem. The most remarkable story is of a small boy of seven in the remote parts of Devonshire, who announced to the company assembled at dinner that a 'very good priest is dead and is just now killed'; though the company laughed and were amused, they heard in seven or eight days that the dreadful tidings were true, and they magnified 'God who so wonderfully awakened the spirit of a young and innocent child to reveal this matter at the very hour.' It is interesting to note that the deaths of both Rufus and Becket were miraculously known in Devonshire at the very moment that they occurred. It is suggestive of a preconcerted means of conveying news which was evidently expected.

The miracles performed by the body of Becket began directly after his death, and were a source of enormous profit to his shrine at Canterbury. The miracles are interesting as showing the type of mind which could believe them, a type which belonged even to the educated men who recorded them. Among the miracles are some performed on animals, including a story of a starling which had been taught to speak; being caught by a hawk it called out the name of Saint Thomas Becket, and the hawk at once let it escape. William of Canterbury accounts for the sudden miraculous power of Becket by propounding the theory that the older saints, having had their fill of glory, retire in favour of the newer martyrs. The true interest of these stories lies, however, in showing that the ideas and customs of that period cannot be judged by the standards of our own times. Belief in the power of the dead, especially the dead god, was still a living force.

A considerable body of folklore and legend grew up round Becket as it did round Joan of Arc. The murderers of Becket came to a bad end according to popular tradition, and the same untrustworthy authority meted out a like fate to Joan's judges. In a folk-tale poetic justice invariably overtakes the villains of the piece, but unfortunately the records, where they are obtainable, show that all Becket's murderers did not die horrible deaths. Hugh de Moreville is known to have become very wealthy, and died fourteen years later quite undramatically.

Joan of Arc

The story of Joan of Arc has been told and re-told many times, usually with a markedly ecclesiastical bias, often with a surprising want of critical acumen and even of historical facts. One of the main sources of our knowledge is the record of her trial before an ecclesiastical court presided over by the bishop of Beauvais and the deputy of the Inquisitor of France.[3] Next in importance is the document of the Rehabilitation.[3] Besides these there are contemporary accounts of her meteoric career, from the time when she sought out Robert de Beaudricourt to inform him of her mission until that day at Compiègne, when she was taken prisoner by the Burgundians.

She came from Lorraine, a district where a century earlier the Synod of Trèves[4] had fulminated against 'all kinds of magic, sorcery, witchcraft, auguries, superstitious writings, observings of days and months, prognostics drawn from the flight of birds or similar things, observation of the stars in order to judge of the destiny of persons born under certain constellations, the illusions of women who boast that they ride at night with Diana or with Herodias and a multitude of other women.' A century after Joan's trial, the inquisitor Nicolas Remy[5] could pride himself on having put to death hundreds of 'witches' in that same district. The backwardness of the country in the time of Joan is shown by the survival of the custom of giving the mother's surname, not the father's, to the children. Clearly then both in social and religious customs Joan's native country still kept many of its more primitive ways.

One of the chief accusations against Joan, and one which she could not refute, was that she had dealings with the fairies. Even her godmother, who should have seen that she was brought up as a Christian, was acquainted with the fairies; and the Sieur de Bourlemont, one of the principal land-owners near Domremy, was married to a fairy lady. It was while engaged in religious ceremonies at the Fairy Tree of Bourlemont that Joan first saw the personages whom she called her Voices, and to whom she gave the names of Christian saints. Her description of the Voices shows that they were certainly human beings and the records prove her words beyond a doubt. It is as yet impossible to identify the two women, but there is a strong indication as to the Saint Michael, for at her trial Joan stated that Saint Michael provided her with her first suit of armour; later, the honour of having been the donor was claimed by Robert de Beaudricourt and Jean de Metz, both of them men of her own country.

Before accepting her, the Dauphin insisted that she should be examined by a body of learned doctors of the Church in order to ascertain if her mission had in it anything 'contrary to the Faith'. Had the whole country been Christian, as we are always led to believe, such an examination would not have been thought of, but if the greater part of the peasantry, especially in out-of-the-way districts like Lorraine, were still Pagan, an examination of the kind was a necessary preliminary precaution for a Christian prince. When Charles appointed her to her high position in the army he told her to choose from his suite the man whom she desired to be her protector in battle. Out of all those courtiers and soldiers she chose Gilles de Rais, the man who nine years afterwards was tried and suffered for his faith as she did. It was at this time that she said to the Dauphin, 'Make the most of me, for I shall last only one year.' A significant remark which showed that, like Rufus and Becket and many other Divine Victims, she knew that her end would come at an appointed time.

Her career of victory is too well known to recapitulate here. Only one comment is needed: if she were regarded by the Pagan men-at-arms as God Incarnate her marvellous power over them is accounted for; they would follow where she led in battle, counting it an honour to give their lives in defence of hers. It was the coming of God in person which put heart into the French troops. The records show that in the eyes of the people she was divine. Article III of the Articles of Accusation states this in plain terms: 'Item, the said Joan by her inventions has seduced the Catholic people, many in her presence adored her as a saint and adored her also in her absence, commanding in her honour masses and collects in the churches; even more, they declared her the greatest of all the saints after the holy Virgin; they set up images and representations of her in the shrines of the saints, and also carried on their persons her representation in lead or in other metal as they are wont to do for the memorials and representations of saints canonized by the Church; they say everywhere that she is the envoy (*nuntia*) of God and that she is more angel than woman.' According to the records she raised the dead, the sick were cured of all diseases by the touch of her garments; and as even professed Christians counted her as almost equal to the Virgin it is more than likely that in the eyes of her Pagan followers she was God indeed. An interesting little sidelight is thrown on the popular opinion of her by Dame Margareta La Touroulde, widow of Réné de Bouligny, Councillor and Receiver-General of the King, who stated at the Enquiry for Rehabilitation that Joan had stayed with her at Bourges and that they had often talked together; she had said to Joan that she (Joan) did not fear to go to the assault because she knew quite well that she would not be killed. Though Joan denied that she was in greater security than the soldiers the remark indicates the feeling towards her. Thibauld de Termes, Bailly of Chartres, was of opinion that what she did was more divine than human. Her own opinion of herself is best expressed in her own words when, in the course of her trial, she boasted to her judges that her Voices spoke of her as 'Johanna Puella Filia Dei'. After the trial her faithful friend and admirer, Gilles de Rais, wrote and staged in her honour a mystery-play, of the type which is known at the present day as a passion-play. At Orleans the great yearly festival, which seems to have originated in pre-Christian times, was given her name, and is still celebrated as the *Fêtes de Jeanne d'Arc*.

Joan was taken prisoner at Compiègne on 23rd May 1430, by the Burgundian noble, Jean de Luxembourg. Three days later the Greffier of the University of Paris sent a summons under the seal of the Inquisitor to the Duke of Burgundy demanding that Joan should be sent to Paris to be questioned by the ecclesiastical authority. It is possible that the Duke did not reply, at any rate his answer has not survived. Joan was not sent to Paris and remained for six months in Burgundian hands. This is a surprising fact, for at that period to capture in battle a person of high rank meant a great accession of wealth to the lucky captor, whose fortune was often made by the ransom. Joan was rich, thanks to the king's generosity, Charles owed everything to her and might be

expected to feel his indebtedness; Gilles de Rais, her chosen
protector, had vast wealth; the city of Orleans, which regarded her as its saviour, was not poor. Yet no trace or
tradition remains that any Frenchman offered to ransom or
rescue her; she was left to her fate. At the end of six months,
when there was still no sign of a French ransom, the Burgundians sold her to the English, and at once the Church,
through the Bishop of Beauvais, demanded that ecclesiastical
trial which had previously been vainly demanded by the
University of Paris.

The trial began on the 9th of January 1431. The court
was composed entirely of priests and monks, presided over
by the Bishop of Beauvais and the deputy of the Inquisitor
of France. She was tried for her faith as the articles of
Accusation make clear. A damning fact was that she had held
communication with 'evil spirits' at the Fairy Tree; in fact,
like John Walsh in Dorsetshire, Bessie Dunlop in Ayrshire,
Alesoun Peirson in Fifeshire, and many others, her connection with the fairies was proof positive that she was not
of the Church. To the modern mind imbued with the present-
day ideas of fairies, such an accusation appears too puerile
to be taken seriously, but the proofs that a connection of the
kind was considered as a capital offence are too frequent to
be disregarded. It must also be remembered that Joan was
not the only witch tried for her faith who surprised the court
by the quickness of her wit and the shrewd intelligence of
her answers. The Witches of Bargarran in Renfrewshire, in
1697, had the same effect on their hearers. 'Several of them
are persons of singular knowledge and acuteness beyond the
level of their station. Margaret Lang did make harangues
in her own defence which neither divine nor lawyer could
well outdo. Their answers to the trying questions put to
them were suprisingly subtle and cautious.'[6]

Though Joan was obviously guided in her answers by
someone in the court, it is equally clear that she was being
guided to her doom. She acknowledged that 'Saint Katherine'
was often in the court directing her how to reply, and that

the saint even succeeded in speaking to her in her room in the prison, presumably through the spy-hole communicating with the next room. In the Rehabilitation, Frère Isambard stated that he was threatened with a ducking because he nudged her and winked at her to indicate how she should reply; the threat so frightened him that he fled to his convent. The priest Loyseleur, who was accused after his death of being an *agent provocateur*, became her adviser. She was often excessively offhand to her judges, treating them consistently with a disrespect unexpected from a Christian towards those in authority in the Church. She often refused to answer a question, saying 'Pass that by'. Sometimes she would say that she would answer a question after an interval of time, two days or four days, or even as long as eight days. At the end of the time required her answer would be ready, showing that she was receiving advice from a distance. Maître Jean Lohier—whose position as a legal or ecclesiastical authority is not defined, he is merely called 'a grave Norman clerk'— it reported to have given it as his considered opinion that had Joan been less positive in her statements she could not have been condemned.

There was a strong feeling at the time that she was not burned, but either escaped or was set free. This opinion was openly expressed and does not seem to have been contradicted by any responsible person. Thus in the *Chronique de Lorraine* it is stated that 'the Pucelle was lost at Compiègne, and no one knew what had become of her; many said that the English had captured her, had taken her to Rouen and burned her; others said that some of the army had killed her because she took all the honour of feats of arms to herself.' The *Chronique de Metz* also discredits the story of the burning, 'Then she was sent to the city of Rouen in Normandy, and there was placed on a scaffold and burned in a fire, so it was said, but since then was found to be the contrary.' Jean Chartier says, 'She was burnt publicly, or another woman resembling her; concerning which many people have been and still are of diverse opinions.' The author of the *Journal d'un Bourgeois de Paris* states that 'many persons who were deceived by her believed firmly that by her holiness she had escaped the fire, and that someone else had been burned and not herself.' It is the same Bourgeois de Paris who speaks of her as 'a creature in the form of a woman, who was called the Pucelle. Who she was God knows.' In 1436 at Arles a man called Veyrier quarrelled with another man called Romieu, because Veyrier declared that the Pucelle of France burnt by the English at Rouen was still alive, a statement which Romieu flatly denied.

In all these statements Joan is always styled La Pucelle de France. Even the English call her by the same title. Thus the Duke of Bedford writing officially to the king speaks of 'a disciple and limb of the Fiend, called the Pucelle.' The *Continuation of the Brut* gives her the same title: 'At that same Journey was take the wicche of Fraunce that was called the Pushell; and she was take alle armd as a man of armys; and by her crafte and sorserie all the Frensshe men and her company Trystid to have ovyrcome all the Englysshe pepull. But God was lord and maister of that victorie and scomfiture, and so she was take, and brought and kept in hold bi the Kynge and his counseill all tymes at his commaundement and wille.' The English regarded her throughout as a witch and therefore believed very naturally that God had delivered her into their hands as a special mark of divine favour to them.

The title of Pucelle of France is peculiar, its exact significance has never been explained. Joan was first the Pucelle of Orleans, but when she quartered the royal Lilies she became the Pucelle of France. This was clearly a definite title, and possibly showed some special relation to the crown. If the king were still regarded as the Incarnate God whose coven was at this time called his Council, Joan might well be the Maiden of the Coven, such as was found so often in Scotland two centuries later. The title Pucelle has otherwise no meaning as it stands.

The years between the trial at Rouen and the rehabilitation must be considered with great care if any conclusion is to be reached concerning Joan as a historical personage. It is so much the fashion to pour floods of tearful sentiment over her that plain facts are not always welcome, but the contemporary evidence is there and has never been refuted.

In 1436, five years after the trial, the herald-at-arms, Fleur de Lils, and Joan's brother, Jean du Lys, arrived at Orleans to announce officially to the town that Joan was still alive.[7] The accounts of the city show that on Sunday, the 6th of August 1436, Jean du Lys, brother of 'Jehane la Pucelle', was in Orleans carrying letters from his sister to the king. He was fêted by the city; the bills for the feast are still extant, and include twelve fowls, twelve pigeons, two goslings, two leverets, besides a considerable quantity of wine. On the 9th of August came the herald-at-arms, Fleur de Lils, bearing letters from Joan to the city; he received two gold coins for the news he brought. On the 21st Jean du Lys on his way back was given money and wine. On the 25th a messenger with letters from La Pucelle was given refreshments. On the 18th of October the herald-at-arms Cueur de Lils (*lequel disoit avoir grant soif*) was well entertained for bringing letters from Jehane la Pucelle.

In July, 1439, Joan's brothers came to Orleans bringing with them the lady whom they claimed to be their sister Joan, now married to the Sieur des Armoises (also spelt Harmoises). The Council of the city of Orleans presented to Jeanne des Armoises 210 livres parisis '*pour le bien qu'elle a fait à ladicte ville durant le siège.*' She appears to have stayed till September the 4th, about six weeks, during which time she must have met many persons who had known Joan of Arc well both personally and by sight. There was Jaquet Leprestre who had presented Joan of Arc with wine in 1429 and again in 1430, and was now supplying the wine for the banquets to Jeanne des Armoises. There was the draper, Jean Luiller, who in 1429 had furnished her with '*de la fine Brucelle vermeille pour faire une robe et une huque.*' In this connection it is well to remember that when Pierronne, a

Breton woman and one of Joan's devoted followers, was tried at Paris she declared that God often appeared to her in human form and acted towards her as one friend to another, and that the last time she saw him he was dressed in a long white robe and under it a *huque de vermeille*. For this blasphemy she was burnt alive, maintaining to the last that she had spoken the truth.

Besides the wine-merchant and the draper, the family with whom Joan had lodged while in Orleans, were alive, and must surely have recognized the Dame des Armoises as an impostor if she were one. Still more important is the fact that Joan's own mother was in Orleans at the time of the visit of Jeanne des Armoises, yet raised no protest. Most significant of all was the discontinuance of the masses said for the repose of Joan's soul, which had been celebrated in Orleans on the anniversary of the burning at Rouen but after the visit of Jeanne des Armoises they were said no longer. In 1443 Pierre du Lys, Joan's youngest brother, petitioned the Duke of Orleans for financial help, pointing out how bravely he had fought in company with his sister, Jeanne la Pucelle, '*until her absence* and since then up to the present time'; which can only mean that he still regarded or feigned to regard the Dame des Armoises as Joan of Arc.[8]

Whether Jeanne des Armoises was an impostor or not cannot be satisfactorily decided, but one fact emerges clearly, which is that Joan's brothers acknowledged her as their sister and Joan's mother did not deny her. Yet in 1450 an attempt at Rehabilitation was begun and lapsed. In 1452 the mother claimed ecclesiastical and civil rehabilitation for Joan; Pierre du Lys seems to have joined in the claim, for he was poor and Joan's wealth had been great. The proceedings dragged on till 1456; in other words, the Sentence of Rehabilitation was not promulgated till twenty-five years after the trial at Rouen. The interesting point is that the relatives, who in 1439 had recognized the Dame des Armoises as the Joan of Arc who had been tried at Rouen, now in 1456 claimed that the same Joan had been put to death by the English in 1431. In both cases money seems to have been the object. The family had made a good thing by exploiting the Dame des Armoises, but they made far more by the exaggeratedly heart-rending details which they collected in order to move the hearts of the judges who presided over the Enquiry for Rehabilitation. The Rehabilitation was for the financial benefit of a family who had already forsworn themselves over the Dame des Armoises.

Most of the judges engaged in the trial at Rouen were dead, and the du Lys family desired that the sentence of excommunication then promulgated should be annulled so that they might inherit the property. In the wildest flights of hatred against the Duke of Bedford and the Earl of Warwick, no one has ever suggested at any time that they desired more than Joan's death, excommincation was not their affair but was a matter for the Church. The Enquiry for Rehabilitation was instituted in order to lift the ban of the Church and allow the derelict wealth to be safely gathered in by Joan's sorrowing relations.

In judging the evidence given at the Enquiry it must be remembered that twenty-five years had elapsed since the events and that the witnesses were speaking from memory. A great deal of the evidence was hearsay, the witnesses continually saying, 'It was common report', or 'It was generally believed', or 'I heard it said.' Some of them spoke of Joan's bearing at the trial and then acknowledged that they had never been present in the court but were repeating what someone else had told them. The executioner's evidence was entirely at secondhand. There were, however, several who spoke from personal knowledge, whose words are therefore of value.

It must be noted that, as in all ecclesiastical trials of the time, the witnesses called were only those who could give evidence on the one side. No one was allowed to speak in favour of the Bishop of Beauvais, the deputy-inquisitor, or other learned Churchmen who had conducted the trial at Rouen, no evidence was admitted which would show that they had acted in good faith; allegations were made against them, but they were not there to refute them, and there was no one to represent or defend them. It was an entirely one-sided Enquiry, which was obviously what the du Lys family desired. To have allowed evidence bearing in the slightest degree against Joan would have defeated the object of the Enquiry, which was to rescind the previous ecclesiastical sentence and so restore Joan's wealth to her mother and brother. The easiest way, and one which in the changed political circumstances was the most desirable and effective, was to charge the judges and witnesses in the original trial with fear of the English and hatred of Charles VII. Yet several of the more reputable witnesses solemnly declared that the court which condemned Joan was not coerced in any way, realizing probably that to admit coercion was to belittle the power of the Church to which they owed allegiance. Nicolas Taquil, who had been an assistant notary at the trial, declared that he saw no English in the court during the examinations of Joan with the exception of her guards; and Guillaume Manchon, one of the chief notaries, stated on oath on two separate occasions, that when Joan complained of the conduct of her guards, the Earl of Warwick was furious with the men and removed them, giving Joan two other guards who appear to have behaved themselves. The evidence of Thomas de Courcelles, professor of theology and Canon of Paris, is particularly interesting as showing the difficulties which a change of government involved; he had been one of the lesser judges at the Rouen trial and had obviously agreed that Joan was a heretic. He now tried to explain away his previous opinion. He remembered well that he never held that Joan was a heretic except in so far that she pertinaciously maintained that she ought not to submit to the Church, and at the end—as his conscience could bear witness before God—it seemed to him that he said that she was as at first, and that if she were a heretic at the first, that is what she was then; but he never positively declared her to be a heretic.

The reason for Joan's resumption of male dress is given quite differently by three witnesses, all of whom claimed to have heard it from Joan herself. Martin Ladvenu reported that Joan wore the dress as a protection from insult, a ridiculous statement if the circumstances of her imprisonment are taken into consideration. Jean Massieu declared that the guards took away the woman's dress and left her only the male costume. Thomas de Courcelles said that he was with the Bishop of Beauvais when the news came that she had resumed the male habit. He accompanied the bishop to the castle, where the bishop interrogated her as to the cause of the change of dress. Joan gave the simple explanation that it seemed to her more suitable to wear a man's dress among men than a woman's. The enormous importance as to the wearing of the male costume is emphasized by the fact that as soon as it was known in Rouen that Joan was again dressed as a man the inhabitants crowded into the castle courtyard to see her, to the great indignation of the English soldiers who promptly drove them out with hard words and threats of hard blows. This circumstance shows the inaccuracy of Ladvenu's statement as to Joan's fear of insult, for it is evident that in the day she could be seen from outside, which would in itself be a protection, and Massieu's words indicate that, like all her contemporaries, she wore no clothes when in bed.

Ladvenu, Massieu and Isamberd were with her to the end, and two of them claim to have been asked to fetch the cross from the church, while Massieu records the making of a little cross of two bits of stick by an English soldier. All three priests were naturally very insistent that Joan died a good Christian, for the Enquiry was set on foot to prove that point. If she were a Pagan she had been rightly excommunicated; but if she had been a Christian the ban of excommunication would have to be lifted. All the priests speak of the cruelty of the Bishop of Beauvais in not permitting her to worship in a church or other shrine, but they appear to have conveniently forgotten that an excommunicated person was not allowed to enter a Christian place of worship. The bishop must have been more kindly than many Inquisitors when he permitted her to 'receive the Body of Christ' before her execution, although she was condemned to the fire as 'idolator, heretic, apostate, relapsed'. A few days after she was burnt, the Inquisitor of France himself preached about her in Paris, and said that she had left her parents, '*accompagnée de l'ennemi d'enfer, et depuis vesquit homicide de chrestienté.*'[9]

If Joan were a Pagan, and in the eyes of her Pagan followers the substitute for the king and therefore God Incarnate for the time being, much of the obscurity which surrounds her life and death is cleared away. She came from a part of the country so well known to be Pagan that she had to be examined by persons whose own Christianity was beyond question before the king could accept her. To announce her mission she went first to Robert de Beaudricourt, agent in Lorraine for King René of Provence, a king whose magical practices would have brought upon him the wrath of the Church but for his high position. Her 'Voices' were called by the names most common among witches, and at her trial she spoke of seeing them 'among the Christians, they themselves unseen'. This use of the word *Christian* again shows that Christianity was not universal. The remark should be compared with the statement by Danaeus[10] that 'among a great company of men, the Sorcerer only knoweth Satan that is present, when other doe not know him, though they see another man, but who or what he is they know not.' It is also reminiscent of the stories of fairies, who were recognized only by the initiates, when in the company of others.

Joan chose for her protector that great soldier who was of her own religion, and who was later tried and executed as a Pagan. She announced that she would last only one year, and during that time she received almost divine honours from the common people, but she was quite aware that at the end of that year she would suffer martyrdom. When the

time came for the sacrifice not one of her friends or worshippers stirred a finger to save her. Throughout her trial
she spoke of her god as 'the King of Heaven' as 'my Lord',
or simply as 'God'; she never mentioned 'Christ' or 'our
Saviour', or even 'our Lord'. It is only in the Rehabilitation
that she is reported to have used the name of Jesus. Many
people vouched for her having cried *Jhesu* with her last
breath, but no one, not even the priests, were very near her
at the end. Massieu, however, stated that she called on God,
Saint Michael and Saint Katherine; in other words, on the
very 'saints' with whom she had been in communication
since her first encounter with them at the Fairy-Tree of
Bourlemont.

She used Christian symbols, such as the cross or the words
'Jhesu Maria', on her letters when they were intended to
deceive. She steadfastly refused to say the Lord's Prayer, a
refusal which in later times would have been tantamount to
confessing herself a witch. She utterly refused to acknowledge
the authority of the Church, though she understood what
was meant by the Pope and asked to be taken to him. She
declined to take the oath on the Gospels, and after much
persuasion and very unwillingly she swore on the Missal.
She treated the ecclesiastics who examined her at Poitiers
with familiarity; when Pierre Séguin de Séguin, Dean of the
Faculty of Theology in the University of Poitiers, asked her
what dialect (idioma) her Voices spoke, she answered 'A
better one than yours', for he spoke in the Limousin dialect.
He then asked her if she believed in God, to which she
replied, 'More than you do.' At the trial at Rouen she treated
her judges with contempt. When asked direct questions
regarding her faith, she invariably prevaricated; thus, when
asked whether she had ever blasphemed God, she answered
that she had never cursed (*maledixit*) the saints; when pressed
to say if she had ever denied God, she would make no other
reply than that she had never denied the saints. One remark
recorded in the Rehabilitation appears significant; it is in
the evidence of Dame Margareta La Touroulde; Joan nar-

rated to her hostess how she had been examined by the clergy at Poitiers, and how she had said to them, 'There is more in the books of our Lord than in yours.' With a slight emphasis on the word *our*, the signification is apparent, otherwise the remark has no meaning.

The wearing of the male costume seems to have had a signification which was clear to the people of her own time though hidden from us. She insisted that she wore it not by the advice of mortal man, and she refused to wear a woman's dress except by the direct command of God. It is impossible to say why so much stress was laid on her attire, as in itself it has never been a capital crime for a woman to appear as a man. Many a lady dressed as a page and went with her husband or lover to the Crusades, more than one woman was known to have donned armour and given a good account of herself in defending her castle. Yet when Joan discarded her woman's dress in prison and put on a man's habit it was the signal for her condemnation. It is possible that the resumption of the dress connoted a resumption of the Old Religion, and that she thereby acknowledged herself a Pagan and the Incarnate God.

Gilles de Rais[11 and 12]

The case of Gilles de Rais is remarkable in that it lends itself, as with Rufus and Joan of Arc, to the cheap claptrap and 'purple patches' of a certain type of writer. The most important publications of the trial of Gilles, those which show a realization of underlying factors, are written by Salomon Reinach and Ludovico Hernandez, both authors being Jews and therefore not swayed by Christian prejudice.

The career of Gilles has been used by the Church in order to pose as the protector of a helpless peasantry oppressed by a brutal overlord; it has also been used by other Christian writers to point a moral; and psychologists have found in it a convenient means of proving or disproving some pet theory. To none of these writers does it seem to occur that the record gives only the evidence for the prosecution. Witnesses for the defence were not admitted and the prisoner had no counsel. As with Joan the court was ecclesiastical and followed the same lines. The accused was pre-judged, and his fate was already decided before he was brought to trial. The strange apathy of Charles VII towards the fate of one of his greatest commanders is as noticeable as when Joan was tried at Rouen.

The chief episode in the career of Gilles was the part he played in the advancement of Charles VII. He was a fine soldier and devoted himself to the cause of the Dauphin as whole-heartedly as Joan herself. He was Joan's chosen protector in battle and he fulfilled his trust faithfully. His rank and military achievements marked him out as one of the foremost soldiers on the French side, and had he not been overshadowed by Joan he must have been credited with having done more than anyone else in bringing about the discomfiture of Charles's enemies. Yet there never seems to have been any jealousy of Joan, such as might have been expected considering their professional relations. When Charles was crowned at Rheims, Gilles, by right of his high position, was one of the knights sent to bring the sacred ampoule of holy oil for the anointing. During the wars with the English Gilles appears to have been a gallant soldier and a faithful partisan of Charles.

His apathy towards Joan when she was undergoing her trial at Rouen is entirely at variance with his character, and is only explicable if both he and she belonged to the Old Religion and he regarded her as the sacrifice.

In the years that followed the trial of the Pucelle, Gilles kept her memory alive by writing and staging the Mystery-play of the Siege of Orleans, which was acted at Orleans by five hundred actors. He spent his time and money in collecting a fine library, including a copy of Saint Augustine's *City of God*; but above all he devoted himself to making the religious services held in the chapels of his castles as sumptuous and magnificent as possible. He expended such colossal amounts on these spectacular services that even his great wealth was diminished. It is an open question whether the reason that he resorted to alchemy was to replenish his coffers or whether he was filled with sheer love of science. Even in those days science had a great attraction, and its votaries were not necessarily allured by the desire for gain only.

The act perpetrated by Gilles which brought him under ecclesiastical censure was that he entered a church fully armed, and thence dragged out Jean Le Ferron, a tonsured cleric, whom he loaded with fetters and imprisoned in one of his castles. But when the king was moved to send the Constable de Richemont to besiege the castle, Gilles set his captive at liberty and paid a fine. This was at Whitsuntide, but it was not till September that the Church summoned him to answer for that offence and an accusation of heresy.

The court was composed almost entirely of priests, the sole exception being Pierre de l'Hospital, President of the States of Brittany. As at Joan's trial the presiding judges were the bishop of the diocese and the deputy of the inquisitor of France. When Gilles consented to appear and refute the charge of heresy, he found that he was accused of sodomy and murder. These were not crimes within the jurisdiction of an ecclesiastical court, and Gilles expressed his opinion in no measured terms. He spoke haughtily and irreverently, calling the priestly judges simoniacs and scoundrels, and saying that he would rather be hanged by the neck with a lace than submit to reply to or appear before such ecclesiastics and judges.

The whole case, when examined carefully and without bias, is seen to be an arranged affair. In one of the items of accusation it is stated that 'the common opinion, general assertion, true reputation, common memory, and public opinion is that the said Gilles has been and is heretic, sorcerer, sodomite, invocator of evil spirits, diviner, killer of innocents, apostate from the faith, idolator.' The evidence produced was clearly concocted, and the priestly court revelled in the details of the horrors which were described—

always in exactly the same words—by the principal witnesses.

It is quite uncertain whether torture were applied or not, but even the possibility of torture does not explain Gilles' sudden change of front. From the haughty scornful noble he became the humble penitent, confessing the wildest crimes with an intensity of self-abasement and a passionate desire for death which are inexplicable if he were moved only by fear of excommunication or of physical pain. If, however, he knew that he was the destined victim required by the Old Religion as the substitute for his royal master, the motive is quite comprehensible. According to his own confession he killed at least eight hundred children; and when Pierre de l'Hospital—the only layman among the judges—was astounded and incredulous and asked him if what he had confessed were really fact, Gilles replied, 'Alas, my lord, you torment yourself and me.' De l'Hospital persisted in his enquiry, 'I do not torment myself, but I am greatly astonished at what you have told me and with which I am not satisfied, and therefore I wish and desire to know the real truth from you about the causes of which I have spoken to you many times.' To this Gilles answered, 'Truly there was no other cause, aim, or intention than what I have told you, and I have told you greater things than this and enough to have put to death ten thousand men.'

De l'Hospital was evidently suspicious of the truth of Gilles' confession for he caused him to be confronted with Prelati, but the two men supported each other's evidence in terms which show that there was collusion. When the examination was over and Prelati was about to depart, Gilles turned to him and said with tears, 'Farewell, François, my friend, nevermore shall we meet in this world. I pray God that he will give us good patience and knowledge, and we may be certain that if you have good patience and trust in God we shall meet again in the great joy of Paradise. And I will pray for you.'

At the end of the trial Gilles was excommunicated for the

second time as a heretic and apostate, and was relinquished
to the secular court presided over by Pierre de l'Hospital.
As Gilles merely repeated the bogus confession which he
had already made before the ecclesiastical court, there was
nothing for the secular court to do but pronounce sentence
of death. His two servants, Henriet and Poitou, had already
received the same sentence, and Gilles now asked as a favour
that they might die with him so that he might comfort and
advise them for their salvation to the last moment and could
set them an example of how to die. This request was granted,
and a further favour was also permitted in allowing Gilles
the choice of the church in which to be buried. Gilles then
made another petition; he asked that on the day of execution
the Bishop of Nantes and all the people of the Church would
walk in the procession which should conduct him to the
gibbet. The whole of Gilles' attitude towards his own death
is inexplicable except on the hypothesis that he died for some
cause which is not openly acknowledged. Is it likely that the
bishop and all the clergy of Nantes would accompany an
excommunicated heretic, a bloodstained criminal such as
Gilles had confessed himself to be, merely because he asked
them to do so? Such an action needs some other explanation
than the usual one of a repentant sinner.

On that October morning, then, the bishop and the clergy
of all the churches of Nantes walked in solemn procession
conducting the three prisoners to their doom. The towns-
people lined the streets or accompanied the procession,
weeping and praying for the condemned. As they moved
through the streets Gilles spoke all the time to his fellow-
sufferers, urging them to be strong and courageous, exhorting
them to look to God for pardon of their sins, and telling them
that they should not fear the death of this world, which was
but a little passing over without which one could not see God
in his glory; that they ought greatly to desire to be out of
this world, where there was nothing but misery, in order to
go into everlasting glory; and that so doing, as soon as their
souls were separated from their bodies, they would meet

again in glory with God in Paradise. Henriet and Poitou thanked Gilles, saying that the death of this world was very pleasant because of the great desire and confidence that they had in the mercy of God and of going to Paradise with their master. Gilles then knelt and prayed, commending himself to Saint James and Saint Michael, especially imploring Saint Michael to receive and present his soul to God. Then true to his promise to set an example to his servants he went to his death before them, they encouraging him to die as a brave and valiant knight in the love of God. He was hanged; and when dead his body was dropped on the lighted pyre below; but before it could be burned it was snatched from the flames, coffined and carried at once to the Carmelite church for burial. The two servants were then executed, but the chronicler takes little interest in them, and dismisses them in a few words, 'And incontinent were the said Henriet and Poitou hanged and burnt, so that they became powder.'

Five years after Gilles' death the king issued a royal ordinance annulling Gilles' debts. In this document no word is breathed of any crimes or offences, mention is made only of the splendid military services which the marshal had rendered at Orleans and Lagny. Ten years after the execution Gilles' estates were restored to his daughter. No slur appears to have rested on the family of Gilles, his daughter was twice married, both times to men of high rank. As she died without children the estates reverted to Gilles' younger brother.

Not long after Gilles' death, his daughter erected a fountain on the spot where her father had been executed. The fountain was dedicated to Sainte Marie de Crée Lait and was much frequented by nursing mothers. On every anniversary of the execution the mothers of Nantes and its neighbourhood beat their children in remembrance of Gilles. These two facts have never yet been explained, yet the first suggests some special power of fertility ascribed to the dead man, differing slightly from the power ordinarily ascribed to the dead. The second is still more remarkable. Ritual beating in commemoration of ritual murder is known in many places, both in ancient and modern times. The maidens of Rome beat each other freely on the anniversary of the death of Romulus, and at the present day in Iraq, on the anniversary of the death of the martyr Hussein, who there ranks as practically divine, flagellants walk in procession beating themselves with iron chains. For Christian examples there was the beating of children on Innocents' Day in commemoration of the children who were killed as substitutes for the Incarnate God. In the *Regnum Papisticum* of Thomas Kirchmaier, written in 1553, there are these lines:

> *The Parentes when this day appears, doe beate their*
> *children all,*
> *(Though nothing they deserve) and servants all to*
> *beating fall,*
> *And Monkes do whip eche other well.*

Until 1845 the Whipping Toms plied their whips freely in the streets of Leicester in commemoration of the massacre of the Danes. With these facts in mind the beating of Henry II in commemoration of Becket and the beating of the Breton children in commemoration of Gilles de Rais assume a strange significance, and point to the fact that in both cases we are dealing with a ritual murder in which the substitute for the Divine King was put to death.

As late as the fifteenth century it was no longer possible for the sacrifice to be consummated by fire at the hands of the populace, but the Church could always be moved to act as the public executioner as had been done in the case of Joan. To the Church both Gilles and Joan were idolators and apostates, both were tried for their faith. Joan was condemned because she could not prove herself a Christian, but Gilles' Christianity was beyond a doubt, and the ordinary laws against vice would have applied with equal force to most of his contemporaries and even to some of his judges. Therefore to ensure his own condemnation he confessed to a series of child-murders which, to anyone who knows the conditions of the country and the period, are absurd and impossible. The evidence offered in proof of the murders was puerile in the extreme, but his bogus confession answered its purpose; Gilles wished to die and he attained his end. His undoubting faith that he would go straight to heaven and the promise of paradise and everlasting glory which he made to his fellow-sufferers are not the mental attitude of an inhuman murderer, but are entirely in keeping with his character as God Incarnate.

Viewed in the light of a Pagan religion the characters and deaths of Rufus, Becket, Joan, and Gilles are reasonable and consistent. In each of them the Dying God was incarnate; Rufus died as the actual king, the other three as substitutes in order that their royal masters might live and reign for a further term of years.

References

Introduction

1. Sinistrari de Ameno, L. M., *Demoniality*, pp. 35, 131, ed. 1879.
2. *Chronicles of Lanercost*, p. 109, ed. Stevenson, 1839.
3. Rymer, T., *Foedera*, II, p. 934, ed. 1704.
4. Chartier, Jean, *Chronique de Charles VII*, III, pp. 40–5, ed. Vallet de Viriville, 1858.
5. De Lancre, P., *Tableau de l'Inconstance des Mauvais Anges*, p. 56, ed. 1613.
6. Bourignon, Antoinette, *La Parole de Dieu*, pp. 86–7, ed. 1683.
7. *Calendar of State Papers*, 1584.

Chapter I

1. Any good textbook on the religions of Egypt, Babylonia and Greece will give many examples of horned deities.
2. Quibell, J. E., *Hierakonpolis*, I, Plate xxix.
3. id. ib., II, Plate xxviii, ed. 1902.
4. Thorpe, B., *Monumenta Ecclesiastica*, II, pp. 32–4, ed. 1840.
5. id. ib., II, p. 249.
6. Danaeus, L., *Dialogue of Witches*, ed. 1575.
7. *Spalding Club Miscellany*, I (1841), pp. 171–2.
8. Boguet, H., *Discours des Sorciers*, p. 137, ed. 1608.
9. De Lancre, P., *Tableau de l'Inconstance des Mauvais Anges*, p. 404, ed. 1613.
10. id. ib., p. 126.
11. id. ib., p. 23.
12. *Wonderfull Discoverie of Elizabeth Sawyer*, C4 rev., ed. 1621.
13. Baines, E., *History of the County Palatine and Duchy of Lancaster*, I, p. 607 note, ed. 1836.
14. Gaule, J., *Select Cases of Conscience*, p. 62, ed. 1646.
15. Stearne, J., *Confirmation and Discovery of Witchcraft*, pp. 28, 38, ed. 1648.
16. Gilbert, W., *Witchcraft in Essex*, p. 2, ed. 1909.
17. Surtees Society, xl (1861) pp. 191, 193.
18. Howell, T. B., *State Trials*, vi, 660, ed. 1816.
19. Rymer, T., *Foedera*, II, p. 934, ed. 1704.
20. Camden Society, *Dame Alice Kyteler*, ed. 1843.
21. Rogers, C., *Scotland Social and Domestic*, p. 276, ed. 1869.
22. Cowan, S., *The Royal House of Stuart*, II, p. 189, ed. 1908.
23. Sharpe, C. K., *Historical Account of Witchcraft in Scotland*, pp. 146–7, ed. 1884.
24. De Lancre, P., *Tableau*, p. 69.

References

25. Howell, T. B., op. cit., vi. 684–5.
26. id., viii, 1035.
27. Goldsmid, E., *Confessions of Witches under Torture*, p. 12, ed. 1886.
28. De Lancre, P., *L'Incrédulité et Mescreance du Sortilège*, p. 769, ed. 1622.
29. Unpublished Record in the Guernsey Greffe.
30. De Lancre, P., *L'Incrédulité*, p. 805.
31. Bodin, J., *Fléau des Demons et Sorciers*, p. 187, ed. 1616.
32. Michaelis, S., *A Discourse of Spirits*, p. 148, ed. 1613.
33. Pitcairn, R., *Criminal Trials*, III, p. 613, ed. 1833.
34. Melville, Sir J., *Memoirs*, Bannatyne Club (1827), pp. 393–6.
35. Pitcairn, R., op. cit., III, pp. 609–10.
36. Quibell, J. E., op. cit., II, Plate xxviii.
37. Bapst, E., *Les Sorcières de Bergheim*, ed. 1929.
38. De Lancre, P., *Tableau*, p. 67.
39. id., *L'Incrédulité*, p. 803.
40. Webster, W., *Basque Legends*, p. 47, ed. 1877.
41. De Lancre, *Tableau*, p. 465.
42. Cannaert, J. B., *Olim procès des Sorcières en Belgique*, p. 44, ed. 1847.
43. Spalding Club Miscellany, I (1841), pp. 120, 127.
44. Bodin, op. cit., p. 190.
45. Day, A., *The English Secretary*, II, p. 23, ed. 1625.
46. Glanvil, J., *Sadducismus Triumphatus*, pt. ii, pp. 296, 304, ed. 1726.
47. Chetham Society, xxxix (1856), *Farington Papers*, p. 128.
48. Calendar of Patent Rolls, 1429–36, p. 10.
49. De Lancre, P., *Tableau*, p. 119.

CHAPTER II

1. Olaus Magnus. *Compendious History of the Goths*, ed. 1658.
2. Sikes, W., *British Goblins*, p. 60, ed. 1881.
3. Day, A., *The English Secretary*, II, p. 23, ed. 1625.
4. *Examination of John Walsh*, ed. 1566.
5. Pitcairn, R., *Criminal Trials*, I, pt. ii, pp. 52–3, ed. 1833.
6. Pitcairn, op. cit., I, pt. ii, p. 163.
7. Pitcairn, op. cit., II, p. 25.
8. Spalding Club Miscellany, I, pp. 199, 121, 125, 177, ed. 1841.
9. Maitland Club Miscellany, II, p. 167, ed. 1840.
10. Law, R., *Memorialls*, p. 27 note, ed. Sharpe, 1818.
11. *Records of the Justiciary Court of Edinburgh*, II, p. 11, ed. 1905.
12. Sprenger, F., *Malleus Maleficarum*, ed. 1620.
13. Remigius, N., *Daemonolatria*, pt. I, ch. xv, 75, ed. 1693.
14. De Lancre, P., *L'Incrédulité et Mescréance du Sortilège*, p. 648, ed. 1622.
15. Bodin, J., *De la Démonomanie des Sorciers*, p. 239B, ed. 1604.
16. Mather, C., *Wonders of the Invisible World*, p. 88, ed. 1862.
17. Bodin, op. cit., pp. 188–9.
18. Wilde, Lady, *Ancient Legends of Ireland*, I, p. 178, ed. 1887.
19. id., *Ancient Cures, Charms and Usages of Ireland*, p. 147, ed. 1890.
20. id., *Legends*, I, pp. 179, 232, 264, II, p. 70.

References

21. Pitcairn, op. cit., III, pp. 604, 611.
22. *Examination of John Walsh.*
23. Pitcairn, op. cit., III, p. 604.
24. Campbell, J. F., *Popular Tales of the West Highlands*, IV, p. 343, ed. 1862.
25. Croker, T. C., *Fairy Legends*, p. 119, ed. 1859.
26. Moore, A. W., *Folklore of the Isle of Man*, p. 41, ed. 1891.
27. Sikes, op. cit., p. 83.
28. Sébillot, P., *Traditions et Superstitions de la Haute Bretagne*, I, p. 75, ed. 1882.
29. Ritson, J., *Fairy Tales*, p. 73, ed. 1875.
30. Chodsko, A., *Fairy Tales of the Slav Peasants*, p. 133, ed. 1896.
31. Campbell, J. F., op. cit., II, p. 57.
32. Pitcairn, op. cit., I, pt. ii, p. 56.
33. *Denham Tracts*, II, pp. 134, 143, ed. 1895.
34. Keightley, T., *Fairy Mythology*, II, p. 161, ed. 1828.
35. Pitcairn, op. cit,. III, p. 611.
36. *Denham Tracts*, II, p. 113.
37. Waldron, G. Manx Society xi (1859), *Description of the Isle of Man*, pp. 126–7.

Chapter III

1. Mather, C., *Wonders of the Invisible World*, p. 160, ed. 1862.
2. Scot, Reginald, *Discoverie of Witchcraft*, Bk. III, p. 40, ed. 1584.
3. De Lancre, P., *L'Incrédulité et Mescréance du Sortilège*, p. 558, ed. 1622.
4. Bodin, J., *De la Démonomanie des Sorciers*, p. 262B, ed. 1604.
5. id. ib., p. 210B.
6. *An Advertisement to the Grand-jury Men of England touching Witches*, p. 8, ed. 1627.
7. Pitcairn, R., *Criminal Trials*, III, p. 63, ed. 1833.
8. Ritson, J., *Robin Hood*, I, pp. v, xxx, ed. 1795.
9. Hernandez, Ludovico, *Le Procès inquisitorial de Gilles de Rais*, ed. 1921.
10. Pitcairn, op. cit., I, pt. ii, p. 52.
11. *Proceedings of the Society of Antiquaries of Scotland*, New Series X (1888), p. 219.
12. Pitcairn, op. cit., III, pp. 610, 613.
13. Danaeus, L., *Dialogue of Witches*, ch. iii, ed. 1575.
14. Sinclair, G., *Satan's Invisible World Discovered*, p. 47, ed. 1871.
15. *Narrative of the Sufferings of a Young Girle*, p. xliv, ed. 1698.
16. Spalding Club Miscellany, I, pp. 114–15, ed. 1841.
17. Pitcairn, op. cit., I, pt. ii.
18. De Lancre, P., *Tableau de l'Inconstance des Mauvais Anges*, p. 125, ed. 1613.
19. Bodin, J., *Fléau des Demons et Sorciers*, p. 373, ed. 1616.
20. De Lancre, *L'Incrédulité*, p. 608.
21. *Full Tryals of Notorious Witches of Worcester*, p. 8, n.d.
22. *Witches of Northamptonshire*, p. 8, ed. 1612.

References

23. *Guernsey Records of Crime.*
24. *Staggering State of Scots Statesmen*, p. 91, ed. C. Rogers, 1872.
25. *La Tradition*, VI (1892), pp. 108–9.
26. Sébillot, P., *Traditions et Superstitions de la Haute Bretagne*, I, p. 189, ed. 1882.
27. Croker, T. C., *Fairy Legends*, p. 125, ed. 1859.
28. *Trial of Isobel Inch*, p. 11, ed. 1855.
29. *Narrative of the Sufferings of a Young Girle*, p. xliv, ed. 1698.
30. Bossard, E., *Gilles de Rais*, p. xiv, ed. 1886.
31. Pitcairn, op. cit., I, pt. ii, pp. 51–6.
32. Baines, E., *History of the County Palatine and Duchy of Lancaster*, I, p. 607 note, ed. 1836.
33. Horneck, A., in Glanvil's *Sadducismus Triumphatus*, pt. ii, p. 487, ed. 1726.
34. *Surtees Society*, XXI (1845), p. 99.
35. Brand, J., *New Description of Orkney*, p. 117, ed. 1703.
36. *Denham Tracts*, II, p. 126, ed. 1895.
37. Strutt, J., *Complete View of the Dress and Habits of the People of England*, I, p. 45, ed. 1796.
38. Boguet, H., *Discours des Sorciers*, p. 102, ed. 1608.
39. Pitcairn, op. cit., III, p. 613.
40. Vallancey, C., *Collectanea de Rebus Hibernicae*, No. X, p. 464, ed. 1770–1804.
41. Kinloch, G. R., *Reliquiae Anticae Scoticae*, p. 133, ed. 1842.
42. De Lancre, *Tableau*, p. 124.
43. id. ib., p. 125.
44. id. ib., p. 135.
45. Bodin, J., *Fléau*, p. 373.
46. Bernard, R., *Guide to Grand-Jury men*, pp. 107, 113, ed. 1627.
47. Glanvil, op. cit., pt. ii, p. 295.
48. *Alse Gooderidge*, pp. 26, 27, ed. 1597.
49. *Examination of John Walsh.*
50. *Proceedings of the Society of Antiquaries of Scotland*, LVI (1922), p. 50.
51. Sharpe, C. K., *Historical Account of Witchcraft in Scotland*, p. 191, ed. 1884.
52. Chetham Society (1845), *Discoverie of Witches.*
53. De Lancre, *L'Incrédulité*, p. 799.
54. Pitcairn, op. cit., I, pt. ii, p. 211.
55. Giffard, G., *Discourse of the subtill Practices of Devills*, p. 18, ed. 1587.
56. Philobiblon Society, VIII (1863–4), *Witches at Chelmsford*, p. 30.
57. *A true and just Record of all the Witches taken at St. Oses*, ed. 1582.
58. *Wonderfull Discoverie of Elizabeth Sawyer*, ed. 1621.
59. Davenport, J., *Witches at Huntingdon*, p. 5, ed. 1646.
60. Chetham Society, XII (1847), *Moore Rental*, p. 59.
61. *Alse Gooderidge of Stapenhill.*
62. Pitcairn, op. cit., III, p. 607.
63. Hornesk, op. cit., pt. ii, p. 490.

References

64. Bapst, E., *Les Sorcières de Bergheim*, p. 95, ed. 1929.
65. De Lancre, *L'Incrédulité*, p. 801.
66. Pitcairn, op. cit., III, p. 604.
67. Lea, H. C., *History of the Inquisition*, III, p. 493, ed. 1888.
68. Camden Society, *Dame Alice Kyteler*. See also Holinshed, *Chronicle of Ireland*, p. 69.
69. Remigius, N., *Daemonolatria*, pt. I, cap. xiv, p. 71, ed. 1693.
70. Boguet, H., *Fléau*, p. 9.
71. Chartier, Jean, *Chronique de Charles VII*, vol. III, p. 45, ed. Vallet de Viriville, 1858.
72. Unpublished trial in the Guernsey Greffe.
73. Boguet, op. cit., p. 104.
74. Cannaert, J. B., *Olim procès des Sorcières en Belgique*, p. 49, ed. 1847.
75. De Lancre, *Tableau*, p. 123.
76. La Tradition, V (1891), p. 215.
77. Glanvil, op. cit., p. 304.
78. Horneck, op. cit., p. 488.
79. Murray, M. A., *Witch Cult in Western Europe*, pp. 279–80, ed. 1921.
80. Russell, R. V., *Tribes and Castes of the Central Provinces*, p. 229.

CHAPTER IV

1. De Lancre, P., *Tableau de l'Inconstance des Mauvais Anges*, p. 398, ed. 1613.
2. id., *L'Incrédulité et Mescréance du Sortilège*, p. 800, ed. 1622.
3. id., *Tableau*, p. 131.
4. id. ib., p. 183.
5. Boguet, H., *Discours des Sorciers*, p. 206–7, ed. 1608.
6. Bourignon, A., *La Vie Extérieure*, pp. 223, 211, ed. 1661.
7. Scot, Reginald, *Discoverie of Witchcraft*, Bk. II, ch. ii, ed. 1584.
8. id. ib., Bk. II, ch. 11.
9. Bodin, J., *Fléau des Démons et Sorciers*, De Lancre, *L'Incrédulité*.
10. Howell, T. B., *State Trials*, IV, 832, ed. 1816.
11. Stearne, J., *Confirmation and Discovery of Witchcraft*, p. 36, ed. 1648.
12. De Lancre, *Tableau*, p. 398.
13. (Among others) *Lawes against Witches and Conjuration*, published by Authority, 1645.—Scot, Reginald, *Discoverie of Witchcraft*, Bk. III, p. 43.—For fuller details with references, see my *Witch Cult in Western Europe*, pp. 86 seq.
14. Bourignon, op. cit., p. 223.
15. Bodin, J., op. cit., p. 465, ed. 1616.
16. Philobiblon Society, VIII (1863–4), *Witches at Chelmsford*, p. 24.
17. Chetham Society (1845), *Discoverie of Witches*, p. B2.
18. Glanvil, J., *Sadducismus Triumphatus*, pt. ii, p. 391, ed. 1726.
19. De Lancre, *Tableau*, p. 131.
20. id. ib., p. 396.
21. (Among others) Mackenzie, Sir George, *Laws and Customs of Scotland*, pp. 47, 48.—Howell, op. cit., VI, p. 683.

References

22. Horneck, A., in Glanvil's *Sadducismus Triumphatus*, pt. II, p. 491.
23. Scot, op. cit., Bk. XVI, ch. iii.
24. Mackenzie, op. cit., p. 48.
25. Highland Papers III (1920), *Witchcraft in Bute*, pp. 6, 12, 13, 22.
26. Horneck, op. cit., p. 491.
27. Boguet, H., op. cit., p. 140.
28. Hutchinson, J., *History of the Province of Massachuset's Bay*, I, p. 31, ed. 1828.
29. id. ib., p. 36.
30. Cooper, T., *Mystery of Witchcraft*, ed. 1617.
31. Mackenzie, op. cit., p. 48.
32. Boguet, op. cit., p. 315.
33. De Lancre, *Tableau*, pp. 195, 399.
34. id., *L'Incrédulité*, pp. 769–70.
35. Cannaert, J. B., *Olim Procès des Sorcières en Belgique*, p. 44, ed. 1847.
36. Spalding Club Miscellany, I, pp. 120, 165, ed. 1841.
37. De Lancre, *L'Incrédulité*, p. 808.
38. Hale, Sir Matthew, *Collection of Modern Relations*, p. 46, ed. 1693.
39. Howell, op. cit., IV, pp. 854–5.
40. Kinloch, G. R., *Reliquiae Antiquae Scoticae*, pp. 124–6, ed. 1848.
41. Sharpe, C. K., *Historical Account of Witchcraft in Scotland*, p. 132, ed. 1884.
42. Highland Papers, III, p. 6.
43. Glanvil, op. cit., pt. ii, pp. 295, 302, 307.
44. id. ib., pt. ii, p. 391.
45. *Scots Magazine*, 1814, p. 200.
46. *Narrative of the Sufferings of a Young Girle*, pp. xli, xlv, ed. 1698.
47. Sinclair, G., *Satan's Invisible World Discovered*, p. 259, ed. 1871.
48. *Witches of Northampton*, ed. 1705.
49. De Lancre, *L'Incrédulité*, p. 38.
50. Cannaert, op. cit., pp. 48, 66.
51. Monseur, E., *Le Folklore Wallon*, p. 84, ed. 1892.
52. La Tradition, VI (1892), p. 106, *Sorcellerie Contemporaine*.
53. Davies, J. C., *Welsh Folklore*, p. 231, ed. 1911.
54. Gaule, J., *Select Cases of Conscience*, p. 63, ed. 1646.
55. De Lancre, *Tableau*, p. 404.
56. Remigius, N., *Daemonolatria*, pt. i, cap. xxxi, p. 131, ed. 1693.
57. Horneck, op. cit., pt. ii, p. 491.
58. Stevenson, J., *Chronicon de Lanercost*, p. 109, Maitland Club, 1839.
59. De Brunne, R., *Handlyng Sinne, ll.*, 9016 seq. Early English Text Society, 1901.
60. Pitcairn, R., *Criminal Trials*, I, pt. ii, pp. 245–6, ed. 1833.
61. Aubrey, J., *Remaines of Gentilisme and Judaisme*, p. 15, ed. 1881.
62. Sikes, W., *British Goblins*, p. 273, ed. 1881.
63. Société des Bibliophiles de Guyenne, I (1879), p. 85.
64. Pitcairn, op. cit., III, p. 606.
65. Spalding Club Miscellany, I (1841), pp. 97–8.
66. Fountainhall, Lord, *Decisions*, I, p. 14, ed. 1759.

References

67. Scot, op. cit., Bk. III, p. 42.
68. Philo-Judaeus, *On a Contemplative Life*, xi.
69. James, M. R., *Apocrypha of the New Testament*, p. 253, ed. 1924.
70. Boguet, op. cit., p. 132.
71. Spalding Club Miscellany, I, pp. 97–8.
72. Phillips, W. J., *Carols*, p. 14, ed. 1921.
73. id. ib., p. 14.
74. id. ib., p. 14.
75. id. ib., p. 14.
76. Remigius, op. cit., cap. xix, p. 88.
77. De Lancre, *Tableau*, p. 127.
78. Pitcairn, op. cit., III, p. 613.
79. Boguet, op. cit., p. 139.
80. Bapst, E., *Les Sorcières de Bergheim*, p. 51, ed. 1929.
81. Glanvil, op. cit., pt. ii, p. 302.
82. Horneck, op. cit., pt. ii, p. 491.
83. Kinloch, op. cit., p. 133.
84. Chetham Society (1845), *Discoverie of Witches*, p. G3.
85. Kinloch, op. cit., p. 121.
86. Glanvil, op. cit., pt. ii, pp. 296–7.
87. Pitcairn, op. cit., I., pt. ii, p. 163.
88. Sharpe, op. cit., p. 131.
89. *Scots Magazine*, 1914, p. 200.
90. Burr, G. L., *Narratives of the Witchcraft Cases*, p. 418, ed. 1914
91. Bapst, op. cit., p. 166.
92. id. ib., p. 167.

Chapter V

1. Bodin, J., *Fléau des Démons et Sorciers*, p. 187, ed. 1616.
2. Boguet, H., *Discours des Sorciers*, p. 131, ed. 1608.
3. Glanvil, J., *Sadducismus Triumphatus*, pt. ii, p. 297, ed. 1726.
4. De Lancre, P., *Tableau de l'Inconstance des Mauvais Anges*, p. 401, ed. 1613.
5. Pitcairn, R., *Criminal Trials*, I, pt. iii, pp.210–11, ed. 1833.
6. Law, R., *Memorialls*, p. 145, ed. 1818.
7. Fountainhall, Lord, *Decisions*, I, p. 14, ed. 1759.
8. De Lancre, op. cit., p. 401, Boguet, op. cit., p. 141.
9. Michaelis, S., *Admirable History of the Possession and Conversion of a Penitent Woman*, ed. 1613.
10. De Lancre, op. cit., p. 408.
11. Black, G. F., *Scottish Antiquary*, ix (1895).
12. De Lancre, op. cit., p. 128.
13. Kinloch, G. R., *Reliquiae Antiquae Scoticae*, p. 121, ed. 1858.
14. *Sadducismus Debellatus*, p. 39, ed. 1697.
15. Klunzinger, C. B., *Upper Egypt, its People and its Products*, pp. 184–5, ed. 1878.
16. Aytoun, W. E., *Ballads of Scotland*, I, p. 35, ed. 1858.

References

17. id. ib., I, p. 9.
18. Cunningham, A., *Traditional Tales of the English and Scottish Peasantry*, p. 251, ed. 1874.
19. *Tryall of Ann Foster*, p. 8, ed. 1881.
20. Grimm, J., *Teutonic Mythology*, 1087, ed. Stallybrass.
21. Baillie, R., *Letters and Journals*, ed. 1841.
22. Bapst, E., *Les Sorcières de Bergheim*.
23. For references, see my *Witch-Cult in Western Europe*.
24. Bapst, E., op. cit.
25. Boguet, H., op. cit., p. 136.
26. *Alse Gooderige of Stapenhill*, pp. 9, 10, ed. 1597.
27. County Folklore, *Orkney*, pp. 107–8.
28. Breasted, J., *Ancient Records*, IV, sections 454–5.
29. Buchanan, G., *History of Scotland*, I, p. 245, ed. 1722.
30. Melville, Sir James, *Memoirs*, p. 395, Bannatyne Club (1827).
31. Pitcairn, R., *Criminal Trials*, I, pt. iii, p. 246, ed. 1833.
32. *Trial, Confession, and Execution of Isobel Inch*, p. 6, ed. 1855.
33. Glanvil, J., op. cit., pt. ii, pp. 297, 303, 307, 311.
34. id. ib., pt. ii, p. 393.
35. Mather, C., *Wonders of the Invisible World*, p. 120, ed. 1862.
36. Pitcairn, op. cit., III, p. 603.
37. Sharpe, C. K., *Historical Account of Witchcraft in Scotland*, p. 96, ed. 1884.
38. Sinclair, G., *Satan's Invisible World Discovered*, p. 23, ed. 1871.
39. Hull, Eleanor, *Folklore of the British Isles*, p. 41, ed. 1928.
40. *Proceedings of the Society of Antiquaries of Scotland*, New Series, X (1888), p. 224.
41. Kinloch, G. R., *Reliquiae Antiquae Scoticae*, pp. 122, 133, 123, ed. 1848.
42. Taylor, J. M., *The Witchcraft Delusion in Colonial Connecticut*, pp. 118–9, n.d.
43. Spalding Club Miscellany, I (1841), p. 192.
44. Scot, Reginald, *Discoverie of Witchcraft*, Bk. III, Ch. 13, ed. 1584.
45. Pitcairn, op. cit., I, pt. ii, p. 218.
46. id. ib., I, pt. ii, p. 237.
47. id. ib., I, pt. ii, pp. 211, 235.
48. Spalding Club Miscellany, I, pp. 120, 124.
49. *Proceedings of the Society of Antiquaries of Scotland*, LVI (1922), p. 50.
50. Glanvil, op. cit., pt. ii, pp. 296, 304.
51. Sharpe, op. cit., p. 132.
52. Horneck, A., in Glanvil's *Sadducismus Triumphatus*, pt. ii, p. 487.
53. *Records of the Justiciary Court of Edinburgh*, II, p. 12, ed. 1905.
54. Grimm, op. cit., p. 1019.
55. Unpublished trial in the Guernsey Greffe.
56. Bapst, E., op. cit.
57. De Lancre, *Tableau*, pp. 123, 400.
58. Pitcairn, op. cit., III, pp. 604, 608.
59. Glanvil, op. cit., pt. ii, pp. 298, 303–4.

References

60. *Wonderfull Discoverie of Elizabeth Sawyer*, ed. 1621.
61. Philobiblon Society, VIII (1863–4), p. 32.
62. Spalding Club Miscellany, I, p. 171.
63. De Lancre, *Tableau*, pp. 462, 464.
64.   id., *L'Incrédulité*, p. 773.
65.   id. ib., p. 796.
66. Pitcairn, op. cit., III, p. 604, 611.
67. Glanvil, op. cit., pt. ii, pp. 302.
68. Bede, *Ecclesiastical History*, Bk. I, ch. 17, ed. Bohn, 1847.
69. Wilde, Lady, *Ancient Legends of Ireland*, I, p. 133, ed. 1887.

Chapter VI

1. Genesis xl, xli.
2. Exodus iv. 2, 17.
3. Numbers xxii, xxiv.
4. 2 Samuel xxiv. 11.
5. Geoffrey of Monmouth, Bk. VII, ch. 3, p. 198, ed. Bohn.
6. D'Ewes, Sir Simonds, *Autobiography*, I, p. 432, note.
7. Gould, S. Baring, *Lives of the British Saints*, I, p. 14. London, 1911.
8.   id., i, pp. 15, 16.
9.   id., i, p. 275.
10.   id., iii, p. 330.
11. William of Malmesbury, *Chronicle*, p. 52. ed. Bohn. London, 1827
12. Ingulph, *Chronicle of Croyland*, p. 3. ed. Bohn. London.
13.   id., p. 11.
14. Roger of Hoveden, *Annals*, i, p. 5. ed. Bohn. London, 1853.
15. William of Malmesbury, *Chronicle*, p. 157.
16. Roger of Hoveden, i, p. 65.
17. William of Malmesbury, p. 143.
18.   id., p. 145.
19.   id., p. 245.
20.   id., p. 166.
21. Ingulph, *Chronicle of Croyland*, p. 258.
22. Higden, R., *Polycronicon*, Bk. VII, p. 411. *Rerum Britannicarum Medii Aevi Scriptores*. London. For Merlin's prophecy of Rufus, see *Ordericus Vitalis*, iv, p. 102. ed. Bohn. London.
23. William of Malmesbury, p. 344.
24. Fabyan, Robert, *The New Chronicles*, p. 321. London, 1811.
25. Stow, John, *The Annales or General Chronicle of England*, pp. 569–70. London, 1615.
26. Froissart, Sir John, *Chronicles*, i, p. 144. ed. Johnes. Hafod Press, 1803.
27. 1 Samuel vii. 9, 10; xii. 17, 18.
28. Hardyng, Iohn, *Chronicle*, p. 360. ed. Ellis. London, 1812.
29.   id. (Proheme), p. 15.
30. Fabyan, p. 661.
31. *Letters and Papers of the Reign of Henry the Eighth*, x (1536), p. 338. Letter No. 798. London, 1887.

References

32. Pitcairn, Robert, *Criminal Trials of Scotland*, I, pt. 2, pp. 211, 218, 237. Edinburgh, 1833.
33. Wilson, Arthur, *Life and Reign of James the First*. 1706.
34. Matthew of Westminster, I, p. 564.
35. Henry of Huntingdon, *Acts of Stephen*, p. 347. ed. Bohn. London, 1853.
36. Higden, viii, p. 584.
37. Polydore Vergil's *English History, Three Books of*, p. 108. Camden Society. London, 1844.
38. Jesse, J. H., *Memoirs of the Court of England during the Reign of the Stuarts and the Protectorate*, ii, pp. 57, 59, 60. London, 1840. See also William Lilley, *Monarchy or No Monarchy*. London, 1651.
39. Murimuth, Adam, *Continuatio Chronicarum*, p. 253. *Rerum Britanicarum Medii Aevi Scriptores*. London, 1889.
40. Genesis xliv. 5.
41. Griffith, F. Ll., and Thompson, H., *Demotic Magical Papyrus of London and Leiden*, pp. 77, 101. London, 1904.
42. 1 Samuel xxviii.
43. D'Israeli, I., *Amenities of Literature*, p. 336. London, 1884.
44. Bruun, D., *The Icelandic Colonization of Greenland*, p. 40. In *Middelelser om Gronland*. Copenhagen, 1918.
45. Scot, Reginald, *Discoverie of Witchcraft*. London, 1665.

Chapter VII

For general information and specific examples of Divine Victims and Royal Gods, see J. G. Frazer, *The Golden Bough*; particularly the volume on *The Dying God*.

1. The principal authorities are Ordericus Vitalis and William of Malmesbury. For detailed references, consult E. A. Freeman, *William Rufus*.
2. Robertson, J. C., *Materials for the Life of Thomas à Becket*, ed. 1858.
3. Quicherat, J. E. J., *Procès de Condamnation et de Réhabilitation de Jeanne d'Arc*, ed. 1841.
4. Bournon, J., *Chroniques de la Lorraine*, p. 19, ed. 1838.
5. Remigius, Nicholas, *Daemonolatria*, Hamburg, 1693.
6. *Sadducismus Debellatus*, p. 59, London, 1698.
7. Polluche, D., *Problème historique sur la Pucelle d'Orléans*, ed. 1826.
8. Delepierre, O., *Doute Historique*, Philobiblon Society, I, 1845.
9. *Journal d'un Bourgeois de Paris*, Panthéon Littéraire, 1838.
10. Danaeus, Lambert, *Dialogue of Witches*, ch. iv, London, 1575.
11. Bossard, Eugène, *Gilles de Rais*, for transcript of the trial, ed. 1886.
12. Hernandez, Ludovico, *Procès inquisitorial de Gilles de Rais*, for translation and commentary, ed. 1921.

Index

Index

Index

Index

Index

Suffolk, 33, 83, 96
Summoner, 70
Sweden, 75, 89, 91, 97, 98, 99, 105
    140, 161

Tattooing, 100
Therapeutae, 110
Theodore of Tarsus, 17, 30
Theory of dying God, 160
Theseus, 27, 28
Thirteen, 68–9, 76–7
Thurso, 81
Tonsure, 39
Transference of illness, 134, 145
Transformation into animals, 142
Tuatha-da-Danann, 55
Twig cross, 187

Ur, 24

Vows of fidelity, 97, 102–4

Wales, 59, 104, 107
Wax images, 71, 130–5, 143
William the Conqueror, 19, 21, 151,
    163, 166, 171
Wincanton (*see* Somerset)
Witch beliefs, 71, 72, 80
Witch descent, 95, 96
Witch vestments, 158, 159, 184, 187,
    190

Yarmouth, 101
Yearly victims, 27, 104, 125
York, 112
Young Tamlane, 126